BY MAHNAZ BADIHIAN

Printed in the United States of America
First Printing 2020
First Edition 2020

10 9 8 7 6 5 4 3 2

Compiled and edited by Mahnaz Badihian
Project manager, Mahvand Sadeghi
Proofreader, Karen M.Magoon, Steven Gray, Shirin B Sadeghi
Page layout, and book design
Youssef Alaoui, Jahid Munshi
Cover design, Mahnaz Badihian
A project of the international literary website Mahmag.org
Front cover art by Mahnaz Badihian. Acrylic on Canvas
Back cover art by Minu Elizabeth Philip

This book is dedicated to all the people in this world.

We need each other for better survival.

Poets, Writers and Artists

INTRODUCTION

I t happened quickly, like a slap to our face, and before we knew it our life changed. It is possible that, to some extent, it is changed forever. It is like a plague involving the entire world. And during this quarantine it was time to read Albert Camus and his famous novel The Plague. "It felt like during the plague in the city of Oran." Written in 1947, it quickly became a bestseller worldwide. I could buy the book for $30 and wait weeks to get it. I decided on the Kindle edition.

Camus wrote:

"Each of us has the plague within him, no one, no one on earth is free from it."

Camus believed that:

"Pestilences have a way of returning in the world. Yet somehow, we find it hard to believe in ones that crash down on our heads from the sky, there have been many plagues as wars in history, yet plague and wars always take people by surprise."

This surprise happened to us in 2020 as a pandemic worldwide. We are still in shock after two months!

While reading the plague and world news about COVID-19, as a poet and artist I decided to collect the feelings of artists and poets and writers from around the world. I started getting submission slowly, but within two weeks the numbers increased rapidly. As I was organizing the submissions and was in quarantine with my husband, I started having fever, significant body ache, coughing, and more. I consulted my daughter, a doctor in Palm Springs who took care of Corona patients. She recommended seeing someone

1

ASAP. I was very sick by now, and it took me all morning to finally see a doctor at 1:00 pm. The doctor said you have Corona without any doubt! She did a Corona test and sent me home with a prescription. The test came back negative after two days, and my condition worsened. I was on combined medications recommended by my two doctors. I was taking a strong dose of Tylenol every 3-4 hours for fever. Probably for only a few hours in those 24 hours was I able to check my email and send thank you notes to those who submitted to this Plague 2020 anthology. While very sick and not knowing where this condition would take me, among all things to worry about was this anthology.

Finally, after ten days, my fever was coming down day by day. I felt the slap of COVID-19 and was surprised by the sudden change in my life and health. But the excitement of this anthology and the responsibility I felt kept me going day and night to compile this book. This is probably the most exciting project in my life. I felt the stress, kindness, hope, and fear that people around the world were feeling. How amazing to see that we are all the same when it comes to disasters like this. We are all members of the big family called the world, as the world-renowned poet, philosopher, and humanist Persian poet Saadi Shirazi, who lived in the 12th century, says in his famous poem: Human Race. The poem is also inscribed on a sizeable hand-made carpet installed in 2005 on the wall of a meeting room in the United Nations building in New York.

"Human beings are members of one body.

In creation, we are made of one gem.

When the conditions in life bring

a limb (member) to pain,

the other members will suffer from the pain.

You, who are not feeling the misery of others,

Do not deserve to be called a human being."

We all are living in a small world, and we should feel the pain of other members of our race.

This collection has an artist as young as 5 years old and a poet as old as 86.
There were almost 2000 submissions, all good art and poetry, but I could
only include approximately 300 for the Plague 2020 anthology. It was not
an easy selection. I read each work several times to decide. I hope this
beautiful and historic collection satisfies readers around the world and
benefits hungry children via UNICEF.

Mahnaz Badihian, May 2020, San Francisco

Shamsiyat Adamu
Nigeria

DARK TIMES

They say pain brings people together,
But fear has us united,
Rivals turned allies,
Wielding our swords against a common enemy.

We've been plunged into dark times,
Where shunning friends and family is how we show affection,
Where social distancing is the sincerest form of love,
Warm embraces replaced by distant nods,
Mothers avoid their children out of love,
And Space is the only way to maintain a relationship.

Suddenly love is two-faced,
And hazmat gear is the new superhero capes,
Isolation has made us all introverted,
Even prayers seem to have failed us,
Our hopes and dreams now an afterthought,
Because all we want now is to live.

Shamsiyat Adamu is from North Central Nigeria. He is studying economics at the National Open University of Nigeria.

Binyam Adenew, *Ethiopia*

Binyam Adenew, *Ethiopia*. Lockdown. Adenew is a CG artist and ASTU Bachelor's degree graduate majored in architectural engineering.

Rodel Agapito,

Rodel Agapito, *Philippines*

Joshua Jardekah Aguilar and Rachel De Vera
Luzon, Philippines

Quarantined

Deafening silence
As I lay on my bed
Woes of finances
Stirs in my head
Nose and mouth covered
My defense beyond our dwelling,
Breathe as my lips sip my sweat
While I do my stealth walking

Days pass by
I rise up, still quarantined
Like chained but not broken
Faith still lingers, the heart is determined

Procrastination seduces me
Thyself indeed a hard foe
Plans like drawn on sand
Slowly washed away by cell media on hand

Prayers were raised
High hopes for assistance
Frontliners were praised
Help and pledges go a distance

Millions inflicted
Thousands lay dead
Mother nature vindicated
True leaders move up ahead
Social distancing strictly imposed
On hard-headed people, this law seems ignored

What a menace to society, I do agree
Stay home stay safe I cried out my plea

No work No pay
Food rations are delayed
What a way the politicians spun our minds to play
How about you? Oh me? Yes, I'm dismayed
Household chores keep my sanity
Quarantine gave way to my time and family
COVID19 an unseen enemy
I pray that soon you'll just be a memory.

Joshua Jardekah C. Aguilar is a Filipino Architect and Educator. The poem is a collaboration between Joshua's mind and Rachel's articulate words. Friends and movie buddies they both have the same birthday but of different years.

Javed Ashraf Ahmed

Javed Ashraf Ahmed

Nazia Ajmal

Nazia Ajmal, Hello Friends, humans are in lockdown. Let's hang out everywhere

Tai OmoAkin /Africana
Nigeria

Lockdown

These days;
Times are long and slow,
I can count every second,
In every tick-tock.
I see birds up and away,
and I envy their freedom.

These days;
greetings are not handshakes.
we even forbid our hands
to touch our own faces.
and I see little 'corona' smiling,
at our mightiness yet helplessness

These days;
you're to pray and fast,
not in worship's house.
you're to work but stay home.
everything that was so important
is close to nothingness.

These days;
we masked our nose and mouth,
not because we're in awe;
the rich and the poor can live together,
In a place called *Isolation center.*
but because we don't want to join them.
These days;
we only want to live another day
and nothing more.

Plague 2020

12

M.S. Alam Alam
Italy

Why Worldwide Lockdown

The whole world is in house arrest
Irrespective of race humankind facing death summon
In the threat of open sword of corona
Poor or wealth, king and people's
They are combating hopelessly.

Years together womanhood harshly molesting without trial
War child dies without identity
They don't know even.

Infectious virus the fate of the nuclear test
Causes environmental crisis
Raise of the level causes the havoc
Set the world in complete threat
The rules of the United nation disappear in the mist
Humankind turned into a self virus.

Human activists again will reunite under the sky
When the corona ceased
All the children will raise their hands.

Secretary-General of the United nation
Could judge for the last time
Justice and compensation against the
The brutal death of coronavirus worldwide
If the end of war child could stop
Women's rape by soldiers since long
Otherwise, the world will witness the more devastating.

Monirul Alam, Bangladesh.

Monirul Alam, Bangladesh. COVID 19 (Quarantine)

Rasme Allat, Indis

Rasme Allat, Indis

Sízà Àmàh
Enugu, Nigeria

House Arrest

A virus has detained the world
And placed everyone on house arrest
This is one profile we never dreamed of having
But tomorrow we can all share the story
From our first-hand experience
A neighbor yesterday
Is distanced from, today
Emily, who lost her brother
Will have herself a private cell
Where she'll wait for death by installment

Yesterday was a promise
To stay away from negative people
Today we have reneged
We'd rather harbor the negative ones
And be at arm's length from the positive

There's an itch to break free from this asylum
To run around the streets
Buy burger from the mall
And play soccer at the beach
But there's something outside there
Scarier than gothic characters
There's a corona crowning every defenseless knight
The choice is ours to make
Between house arrest and mass burial

*Sízà Àmàh is a poet, actor, and travel writer. He lives in
southeastern Nigeria. He is a fellow of the Aba Poetry Club*

Aliza Amatya, Nepal.

Aliza Amatya, Nepal. Indelible 2020. BA Tribhuvan University. Fashion and Design.

Indran Amirthanayagam
Rockville, MD,USA

Time Present

There will be time, the poet said, to murder
and create, and I grew up thinking I would stop
the sea as well as bake a few thousand cakes
that sing and dance on the tongue, and murder
only cockroaches and snakes. But I cannot sift
and parse, make concessions and compromise
for the rest of my days. I must choose a path,
be true to some plan, show resolve, and purpose.
If not I would be deemed mercurial, humored,
a human folly not a computer or a stable figure,
a steady captain on deck to recite O Captain!
My Captain! over the raging sea. But help
me out, may I still kill the roach while arguing
for sustainable living, long-term conservation
of the ecosystem? If they are unseen, insidious,
what options do I have but to bleach microbes
who wishes to invade me? They do not come coated
with love, flapping wings of turtle doves. But
perhaps they offer me release, an early exit from
this stifling, overheating fishbowl, once a gentle
trade-winded cul de sac? Claptrap. Remind
me of the Big Bang, flaming rocks the size
of the Empire State, and the carnivorous,
malevolent Tyrannosaurus. Let me go back
to dust with that earlier predator. How easy
to pull off the calm veneer, especially when
trafficking in words. Damn this. I am going
for a walk. The sun is shining, and the winds
are quiet today. Who knows when the first
hurricane of the Atlantic season will roar

through the COVID-infested atmosphere.
get communing with nature when I can.
but keep distant from neighbors. Not
a problem: the grand illusion, faith
in tomorrow, conserving one's health.
I must keep that idea circulating
for babies arriving today, kids waiting
for treats at the next Halloween,
and older men and women whose fronds
were blessed yesterday on Palm Sunday
with the gift of memory, during this
COVID year whose collateral benefits
include digging into the attic of the mind,
finding photographs, sharing them
with any household members, and online.

Mehedi Amin, Bangladesh

Mehedi Amin, Bangladesh. Mehedi Amin is an architect and artist. Currently working for the Bangladesh Government at Country Wide Rural Market Infrastructure Development Project (CRMIDP).

Asma Anwar/Pakistan

Virus

تھا آخر کا سردیوں
اور گرمیوں کا آغاز بھی
دھانے اس کے دنیا گول اس
جس دھانے میں آباد تھی

It was the end of winter
And start of summer
At that border of this round world
Where i was living

پھولوں کو پھر سے کھلنا تھا
اور موسمی پھل بھی بدلنا تھا
جاڑے نے تھے جو جھاڑ دئیے
ان پتوں کو پھر سے لگنا تھا

Flowers had to bloom again
And seasonal food had near to change
Which had fell down by cold
Those leaves were near to regain

تھے والے لگنے بھی میلے
رحمت کا موسم قریب تھا
میرے دیس کے باسی مصروف تھے
امیر تھا چاہے کوئی غریب تھا

Festivals near to start
Blessed season was at border
All citizens of my country were busy
Either rich he was or poor

پھر یکایک ساری فضاء بدلی
سنا ہے کوئی جان لیوا وباء آئی
موسم جیسے ٹھہر گیا منظر سارا بکھر گیا
ہے بھاری کیسی جانے ,ہے طاری سکتہ پہ شے ہر.

Then suddenly whole scenery changed
I heard a deadly disease came
The season had struck, and scenery had removed
Everything is struck. Don't know what calamity it is..?

Adrian Arias,

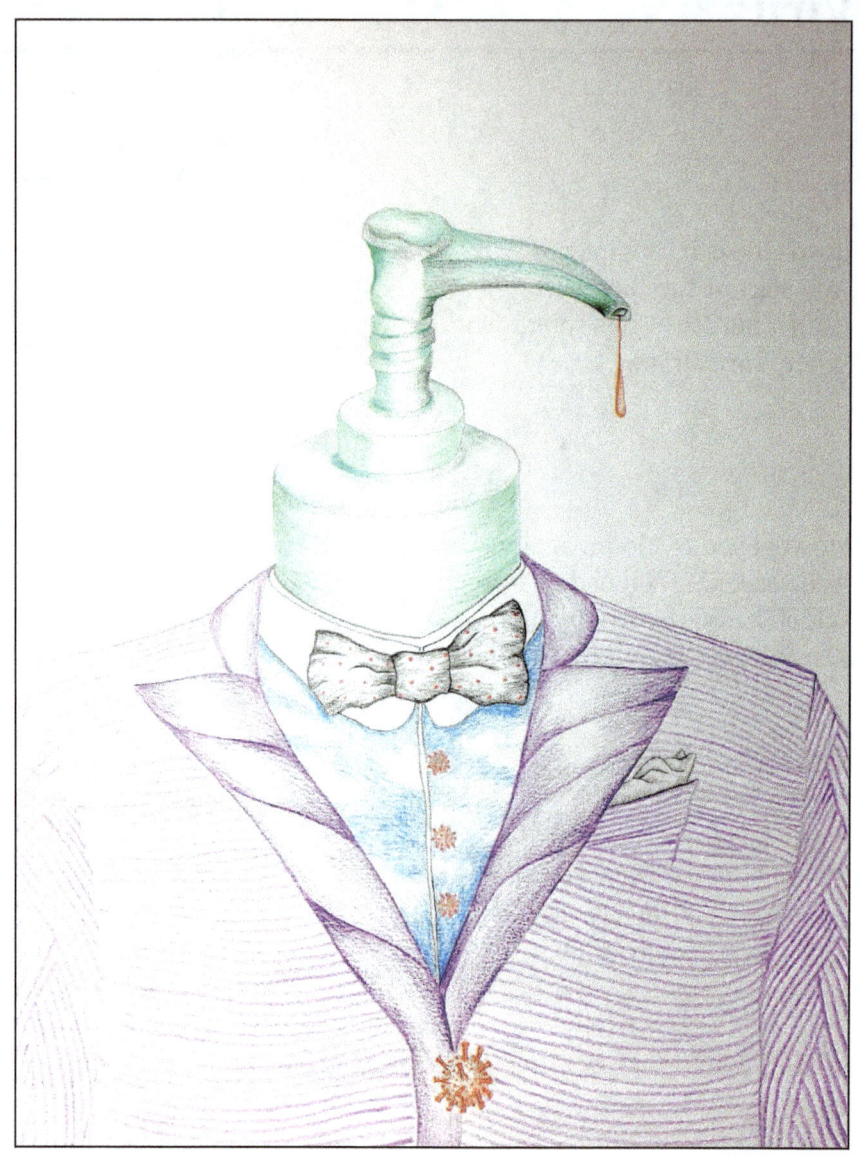

Adrian Arias, *Peru/US*

Adrian Arias
Peru/US

Love in times of CoronaVirus (3)

A spider runs across my face very slowly. It touches every part of my face, and I am petrified. I don't know what to do, and at the same time, I enjoy it. I can't touch my face myself. It's forbidden. So I let the spider go its way, I let her touch me. When it reaches my chin, the spider leaps toward the window and sneaks through a crack to go outside. I want to accompany her, but I cannot. It is prohibited. I'm going to the bathroom. I look at my face in the mirror, I want to touch myself and I can't. I miss the spider.

Poem of the day in times of Pandemia

The still clouds look at us in silence
the lake water murmurs its calm
buildings close their eyes
the dry tree speaks to me
"Come sit down for a while to contemplate life."
I sit down and understand
that everything looks like yesterday
but it is not like yesterday...

Love in times of CoronaVirus (4)

This morning I woke up sad. I had a dream about the end of the world. I wrote it in my dream notebook. Then I made myself a coffee and wondered when I would hug again? I checked my supply amount, all good for now. I looked out the window and knew it was true, and they are free as before. There was a deer in my garden, along with two raccoons and an opossum. Then a hawk came and stood on a branch of my tree, that tree that was never mine, that never will be, like this earth and this planet, all on loan. I wanted to go out and have my coffee taking a closer look at the animals that are now free in the streets, but it is prohibited. I decided to go back to bed to continue dreaming.

Adrian Arias is an American visual-poet born in Peru.

Kirill Gera Arkadyev

Kirill Gera Arkadyev, *Moscow, Russia.* **Dirt. Arkadyev was winner of the international Festival of Abstraction Art in St Petersberg.**

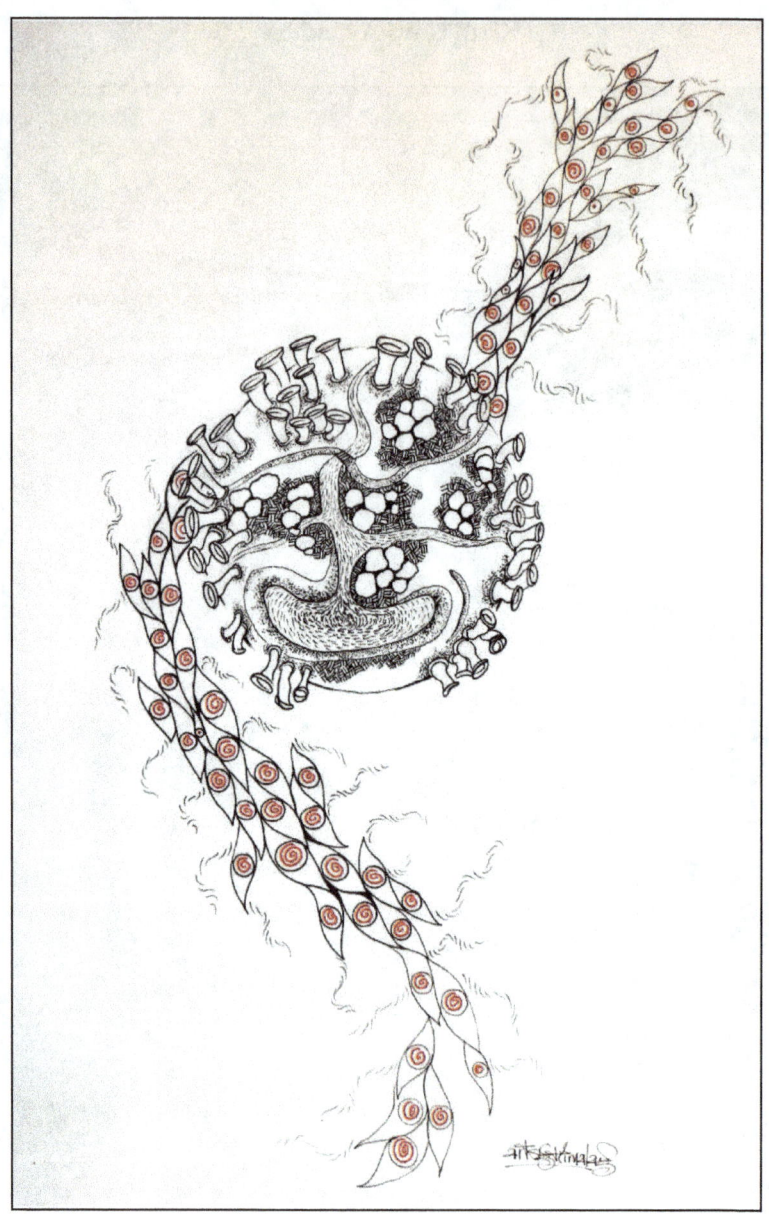

Artsyhimalay HR75
EARTH: Thanks Corona
You helped me in healing…
They troubled me a lot,
But I still love them.

Irfan Aslam
Lahore, Pakistan

Shoe Shiner on a Lahore Road

A box hanging on his shoulder
Full of cheap polishes and shoe brushes
On a deserted high-end market road
What does he look for, this youngster
When Lahore is empty of every outsider
The heavy-footed walk of the outsider of outsiders
Still creeps on a sleepy way as he reclines to one side
Fear of the unseen subdues the city's messy pride
Offices, shops are shut, streets empty
A constant seeping fear is up, and life is down
This city is turning into a ghost town
Who would get his shoes polished
And give this boy rupees twenty
And if he pockets the nominal money
That he so much desires
Who knows he might get infected
By the killer coronavirus
But he is already one of the rejected
His life is already infected.

Mahnaz Badihian
USA/Iran

Plague of 2020

Came crueler than the criminals
more robust than a cannon and a gun
more significant than the world economy
and redder than Stalin's red army

Corona came with a lesson for all
more important than
the experiences of Rumi
bigger than Plato's advice

Scared us away to hide
in the holes of our houses all alone
fear of hunger grows in us
more significant than the fear of world hunger

We rushed to fill our shelves
with bread and cheese
fill our bowls with food and seeds
and attack the shops filled with
fear and despair

Corona had ordered us
to empty the streets
to stop our jobs
and build the fear of death

Like a sun ray did not differentiate between
black and white
poor and rich
powerful and powerless

Came to relive the suffocated breath of nature
to calm the wounded plains
to revive the sick nature from pollution

Corona had come to strip us naked
of pride, prejudice, and greed

It was so small
that wasn't visible
and so big that every day
carried hundreds of people with him
to bury them in a mass graves

مهناز بدیهیان

آمد سنگدل تر از جانیان
قویتر از توپ و تفنگ
برجسته تر از اقتصاد جهان
و خونین تر از ارتش سرخ استالین

کرونا آمد با درسی برای همگان
بزرگتر از تجربه ی مولانا
مهمتر از نصایح افلاطون

وحشت زده امان کرد
پنهان شدیم در پستوی خانه ها
ترس از گرسنه ماندن در ما رویید
ترسی قویتر از گرسنگی مردمان فقیر
حمله کردیم به مغازه ها
مغازه هایی پر از ترس و دلهره
پر کردیم گنجه هارا از نان و پنیر
کاسه ها را از دانه و آذوقه

کرونا آمد تا با یک فرمان
خیابانها را خالی کند
کارمان را تعطیل

با دستانی که سرخ و سیاه و سفید نشناخت
فقیر و ثروتمند نشناخت

آمد تا نفس طبیعت را آرام کند
تا دشتهای زخمی را فرصتی برای التیام
آمد که رخصتی دهد به ساکنین این جهان
عریانمان کند از غرور و ولع

کرونا آنقدر کوچک بود که دیده نشد
و آنقدر بزرگ که هرروزه با خود
دسته دسته می برد انسانها را
به گورهای دسته جمعی

Shruti Badoni
India

Quarantined

Quarantined,
I felt
restless
after taking more than
Five days of rest,
at one go;

It was as if
all I had ever wished for
was now right in front of me,
so much time
to focus on me
in isolation,
without the interference
of anybody else
at all
in a row;

Day 1,
I bloomed
& pampered myself;
Day 2,
I was happier
to have more time
& do everything I desired of
in the year two thousand twelve;
Day 3,
I was habituated
to the long hours of sleep and plenty of spare time to repeat,
the same 2-day old routine;

Day 4,
I wanted to go out
for some fresh breath of air
but was restricted
to a home arrest,
which seemed a little unfair,
Day 5,
I cried a little inside
& stood at my balcony,
for 85 minutes straight
for I needed
the fresh chunk of oxygen
& the moving world
in front of my eyes, which was now shunned;

Quarantined,
we are all aware
it is for us,
& the least we can do
is follow the rules
but,

Quarantined,
I have never felt
so restless & finicky,
after having all I ever wished for
in front of me
on a platter, serving
134 crore people
concomitantly.

Shruti Badoni is a 21-year-old girl pursuing Economics Honors from Delhi University. Apart from having a keen interest in writing, she is also an avid traveler, reader, & economics enthusiast who has big love for good food and the latest ongoing fashion trends!!

Puspa Bakhunchhe
Kathmandu, Nepal

I Went to My Terrace Today

It took me a while to realize
I can see bees and butterflies
Birds chirping around
Flying like they don't want to land to ground
Bright sky and fresh air
Also, the Himalayas too near

My cell beeps in the meantime
Notifications flooded online
World suffering from pandemic COVID-19
Thousands in bed, hundreds in a coffin
With due respect to heroes working frontline
May you heal everyone, sparkle hope & shine

Take a deep breath
Stay home, stay safe

Paul Balam *Kampala, Uganda.* **Sudden Change**

Elhaam Banaie, *Iran*

Bijan Baran
Iran/US

Venceremos

Love in the age of Corona
Battle with the dark
Man will conquer it.
The hidden attack on man's health
The defense line – nurses, physicians, drugs, labs
Not the army and armament of destruction
Medical care, in-hospital services,
Away from family
We are choosing bread over life.

Workers with empty table and unemployment
Buying bread is hard.

The rule of cold silence
Corona despotism censors people's interaction.
Electronic monitoring with facial feature and degerming contacts;
He locked down streets, cities, airports.
Separating the infected people

Death in solitude
Burial in solitude
The absence of groups grieving
Life grafts to souls
Graveyard saturated with the dead
Life and death and living are not predicted.
The age of breaks and crevices in the world pyramid of power.

Tomorrow makes a path for us
In our win
Human rights will prevail all over the world.

Again, the spring will be the garden's guest
Four o'clock- mixed red, yellow, white
On top of a green sphere
connected to the Sun.
Neighbors leave home to work
Bazaar, schools, cinemas, stadiums reopen;
A man shakes hands with a man
They become kinder to our species, animals, and environment.

Poetry is the source of consolation and caring
During the corona pandemic
The corona generation
Will tell their children of social distancing.

*We win, in Spanish

Chris Barras
Cumbria, UK

Corona Update

He swiveled around
And started to speak
And the tongue was all covered in slime
And out slipped words slimy and sticky
And the belly heaved like toads on a lily
And he opened his hand and flung them further
And the pinstripe suit flapped, like reusable bags trapped, on
barbed wire
And words came faster like hail in the rain
Then things took a   sinister   slide
And his eyes opened wide and invited you in
And he lowered his voice, so you have to lean nearer
And spoke words so precise like a political speech
And words off the tongue with a rhythmic beat
And all hope and reason away were beaten away
And that what was said dissolved the walls and the floor
And fear spread like a global pandemic on skates

Then came a silence you could hear a fairy
dance on the head of a pin
leaving you alone with
just you in your head

The chair swiveled taking the man back to his screen
his chart and projections working away on viable futures
working out how to get you out of your head

*Chris Barras is a UK poet living in Cumbria, living between the sea
and mountains. His work is influenced by people and where he lives*

Virginia Barrett /US

Collection Day

We are feeling the universe with giant gloves
which grow each night covering

the cosmos, as one covers their face
when caught by surprise or an overwhelming

grief. Cloud-shadows move and don't
run; walking trees make their way closer

to stars while we sleep, swinging on
limbs. From the window, I watch a woman

wheel a dog in a carriage on the sidewalk
as a man pushes a shopping cart down

the middle of the dead-end street. She's
shouting at him across space between

them, over the rattle of the metal cart, piled
with plastic garbage bags full of empties.

They vanish from view, become barely
audible: gone. I put on my mask and go

outside. After collection, blue recycling
bins stand like bodies congregating

for action yet to begin. I breathe through
the tight weave, watch the light salvage

wreckage from the sun; I am too seldom
at the ocean to hear the murmuring of shells

Jormaine Pascual Bastian. *Baguio City, Philippine*s. **Salutation and greetings to our frontliners**

Saumya Bhalerao *India,* **At the Time of Corona.** Oil on 10"x12" canvas board

Scott Bird
San Francisco, USA

Hear and Now

I heard three coyotes howling
on Corona Hill last night
I heard the red-tail hawk
scream sweet rejoicings today.

I can hear the flow of water
and the flutter of winged
creatures that twitter and
pollinate the budding
thought flowers along their way.

I heard that the fish &
dolphins came back to the
Venetian canals and then
I heard that the ducks and swans

reclaimed the fountains in
plazas across Rome.

I heard that people sang
a collective aria in the opera
house of alleyways from the windows
of their quarantined homes.

I heard that China's carbon
emissions have been reduced by
100 million metric tons.
I heard that Supervisor
Preston called for the city of San

Francisco to allow for vacant
developments to be offered up for
folks are living on sidewalks and in tents.
I heard we might get a break on rent?
I heard someone say, "I think
Mother Earth is doing a 'deep cleaning.'
like we occasionally need
to do in our own homes.'"

I hear the skies growing faint
again as one airplane after
another ground itself. I hear
the silent void of new adventures
emerging from the dulling roar.

I hear the tinnitus ring in my
ears until it fades to all these
sounds of the real world which
surrounds us all.

Please, for the love
of life inside, tell me
you hear it too

Scott Bird is a San Francisco poet, musician, and songwriter.

Kranti Bhoy Maharashtra, India

Kristina Brown, US

Under the CoronaVirus Sun/Couples

1.
Couples
under the coronavirus sun:
Some heat up
and others
cool down.
Some move closer
others apart.

2.
I think of my friends who are sheltering alone.
but then I find out many of them aren't.
not anymore.
not since the coronavirus sun rose.

They've chosen a pandemic partner:
one person to play with
and allow in their house.
they may be lovers.

Or they may always stand six feet apart.
but they are together.

Kristina Brown is a poet, painter, and writer who grew up in Japan and has lived most of her adult life in San Francisco. She often writes about what people will and won't do for love. She likes to take photos of the beauty that is unexpected.

Samuel Chaka

Nigeria, Plateau State

Staring

Staring and staring as often as not at the ceiling;
Looking as if one has lost a shilling,
And found six pence, trapped in suspense.
Gut feeling lost in translation.
There comes a day of quarantine

And the day of isolation.
These were the days of hunger and depression.
I saw purple shadows that looked
Like dawn, noon glare, hazy afternoons
Sunset throwing this golden shadow over everything.

My voice mimicked the word it was conveying,
Trailing off into nothing.
Straining to hear the infant inhale
And exhale of my young lungs.
Caused filled the air as my breath
returned to the moments unspent.

Yes, as I am, the world is scared to death, ill-health.
But what could be more new,
Breaking new ground,
Then the 7 o'clock news.
Coronavirus, a deadly pandemic disease;
Stood center stage in the crosshairs of history,

And ceased the corridors of power.
Putting the cat among the pigeons.
Social distancing the order of the day;

Washing of hands and sanitizing of homes,
All-day, everyday like the Sabbath day.

Nevermore shaking, hugging and kissing between lovers and
friends,
As not to be found guilty of coughing and sneezing
on the day of reckoning at the receiving ends.
Our homes like the four corners of a prison cell lockdown,
Like a cellphone, our shops' shutdown.

Wearing our hearts on our sleeves,
Practicing patience waiting for the other shoe to drop.
The masses with hat in hand;
Pleading for support with their boots on the ground,
But the government's donation is like a drop in the ocean.
Covid-19 is another nail in our coffin.

*Samuel Chaka is an actor, a writer, a performing poet, and a spoken
word artist. Best known to be Pagez, the last born from a family of
five. From Jos, plateau state, Nigeria.*

WORLD IS LOCKDOWN

Kollol Chakrabarty, *Sylhet, Bangladesh.* **World is Lockdown.** Kollol is a drawing teacher in Jalalabad Cantonment English School & College, Sylhet with a Masters in Management & Diploma in Fine Arts & Library Science.

Gilang Chandera, Indonesia All is Well

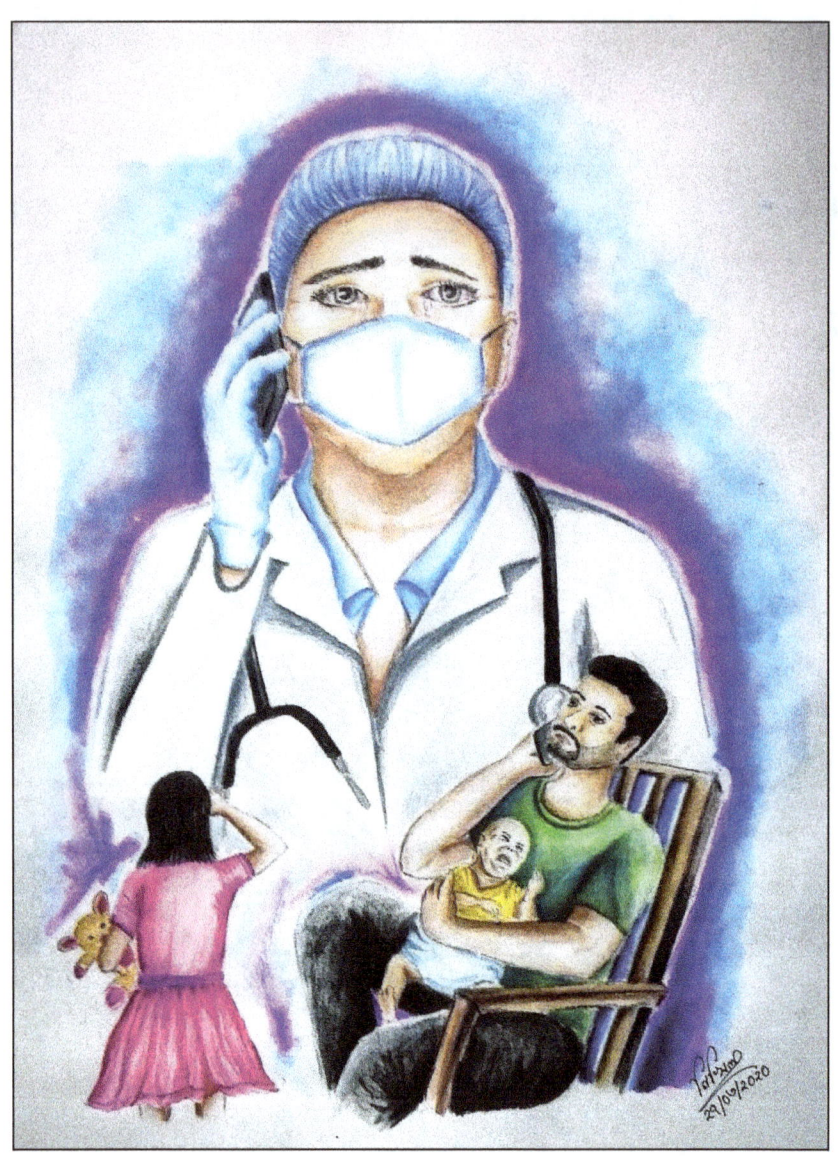

Nikhil Chetia India Family Versus Duty

Michael Chukwudi
Nigeria

The Sorcerer's Voice

Out of curiosity
I wanted to travel to a far world
Travel to Camelot
To ask for the COVID cure
Who knows Gaius may have found it
Merlin may have used magic to forge the vaccine

But will the present Arthurian Government
Allow me to enter the Aso gate
To display my vaccine to be tested
Perhaps, I'm not one of the elites
But I will use the Merlinian way to save the world
The world needs me like Merlin

It is my destiny to save the world
The world is shattered
I will not allow Morgana to destroy the world
Instead, the world will know of my hidden magic powers
COVID will not win this war; COVID will be defeated
The world must be healed

Michael Chukwudi Ikegwu graduated with a First Class Bachelor's degree from the Department of Applied Biology, Ebonyi State University, Abakaliki, Nigeria. His writing includes poems, fiction, essays, and short stories. He was published in Water Anthology, India, African Brave Voices and Poetry Journal 60. He's a visionary writer who sees things as they happen in society and writes them.

Samaira Chy, 10 years old

Ravi Teja Civil India

Feelings Revealed at the Time of Death

There came a million dead bodies in a stream
I thought it was nothing but a bad dream

As I woke up and founded it real,
My heart shattered with fear.

Hundreds turned thousands and thousands into lakhs..,
I felt that we're in this era's climax

No place left in the burial ground,
Someone, please do kill this deadly hound

Don't go out., Never in a hurry
This is the panic situation that one needs to worry about..

Think about our families and those innocent kids
Their lives aren't in an auction, and they're not your bids

Never come out from your home,
Because that's the only way to survive this syndrome.

Keeping beside all this terror and Fear
The only thing in my heart is to hug you tight, my dear

The death might come, or it leaves.,
But remember I'll go with you to heaven and hells

Linda Crate
USA

Sacrifice the Rich

sacrifice the rich
this dystopian nightmare
seems like something
out of a horror novel,
but I am ready
to surrender to the rich to the beast
if that's what they need to devour;

they've put our lives on the lines
and they don't seem to care
that we're essential to those who love us

i guess calling us sacrificial lambs is a little
too on the nose because that's exactly what we are to them—

i am ready for the nightmares to end,
and the dreams to begin
the greed and corruption of men disgust me

in the end, we are all human
each of us has a song and a purpose and heart full
of music and life vibrant as the sun and the moon—

rich men only care about money,
if the world needs a sacrifice;
then it's my recommendation that we send the
politicians: all of them

we need a world with dreams because we've already had
enough nightmares.

John Curl
USA

Cloud Castles

After all this blood, here we are, still
torn in this crisis of destruction and
delusion. At a time like this, as
pestilence stalks every street, how
can we even think of a celebration?

Remember that hazy
summer day we lay
side by side in the grass
gazing lazily
into the clouds, tell me
what do you see?
A dolphin jumping
through a wave
a swaying palm tree
a field of corn
a rhinoceros horn
wind and rain
the shapes change
a swooping bumblebee
a raging storm at sea
a crimson bird
soaring along the horizon
a frowning clown
an angry crowd
a thundering herd of bison.
Look up into the
sky, into the clouds,
Tell me what you see.

Grim masks in crowded dungeons
prisoners whispering forbidden
thoughts forever unfinished.
Midwives hugging bleeding infants
orphans holding endless wakes
widows seizing desperate moments
windows shattering lost childhoods
concrete collapsing bridges and dams
toxic water gushing through neighborhoods
broken priests torturing war dogs
everyday terror and plunder.
boys murdering men murdering women
forests blazing animals fleeing
all the great-grandchildren scream
the gangster banker regime
the loathsome empire's
last bitter crimes drip dripping
dark splatters of blood
on the last rotting dreams
clotting in the last gutter.
None of this will
ever be forgotten.

Yet it is written:
Invincible regimes collapse
all-powerful empires
swept away to nowhere.
New civilizations arise
from the earth
with a kiss.
The clouds change.
The moment of
the celebration is to be.

Remember that hazy
summer day we lay
lazily in the grass,
gazing up into

the sky, tell me,
what do you see?
lovers in a filthy jail
the rings on a tiger's tail
salmon creeks
flamingo beaks
grazing gazelles
buddha bells
flowering Joshua trees
sunrise over turquoise seas.

Ralph Benedict M Dela Cruz. Philippines

Munna Dey
Bangladesh

In The Realms Of Fear

Call it a curse to mankind
or a blessing to nature
whatever you sow, keep in mind
so shall you reap in the future!
Devil corona decides death
weaker ones losing their breath
the virus now wears its crown
while there is a curfew in the town!
All the doors shut, windows ceased
and neighborhood noises decreased
social-distancing, are we told to practice
to stop the disease prognosis!
The virus is spreading like fire
death tolls are rising higher
the government expects more in days or few
the situation is going to get
much worse before it gets better.
Still for our freedom from
home-quarantine is what matters!
We are paying for our wrong deed
warnings and precautions are paid no heed
still, there is only one hope in thee
shall the man-kind heel and the bug kneel!!

Ib Dada-dDsu United Kingdom. **Couple in Lockdown**. Born in western Nigeria on the island of Lagos, Ib attended Design Auchi Polytechnic and Telford College of Art in England. He was resident of the Artist National Gallery of Art Nigeria

Dsk Dharmasena
Anuradhapura, Sri Lanka

Life in a Lockdown

Locked - down at home,
Life floats aimlessly, future's bleak,
This intolerable confinement.

Thrown back to the past is past,
Entangled me in a stream of thoughts.
Nearly felt how Anne Frank had been suffering
Years back,
In her two long years of hiding – Impossible!
Tears run down my cheeks for the young girl.
Then why can't I paddle this suffering till tomorrow?

Suddenly a Buddhist monk appears on television,
"Are you unhappy in the lockdown?"
"It's time to prepare yourself for the eve of your life"
A sudden realization of life,
Determine to accept life,
With compassion.

Alann De Vuyst, Belgium/Residing in Sri Lanka.

Lockdown in Serendib, 2020

Sarita Dongol, Nepal. Let Nature Make its Own Masks. She was awarded the special prize in National Art Exhibition in 2009, a Gold Medal from Arniko Yuwa Sewa Kosh, 1rst prize in Human Happiness Art competition, and the JANAMAT Award Kathmandu, Nepal.

Moinak Dutta
Kolkata, India

Love in the time of Corona

I yearn for your simple touch on my skin,
A simple tap of your fingers, quick and playful,
Alas! We stay under one roof and yet
Can't even get close enough to you
To get the fragrance of your perfumed hair,
Can't run my fingers through your black tresses,
Or put a kiss straight on your soft and glossy lips;

Death, we both, know is lurking around
Like a shadow,
Mere sneezing or coughing,
It could lay its hold upon us,
Without we even knowing,
Like a profound secret;

So I look at you from our socially distanced positions,
Three feet we measure by tape, precise,
Our lovemaking, we have surrendered at the feet of Death.

Moinak Dutta is a published fiction writer and a poet, having got two literary & romantic fictions to his credit, namely "Online@offline," "In search of la radice." Many poems and short stories written by him found their way into several dailies, magazines, journals, ezines, and anthologies. He lives with his wife, son, and a pet dog.

Hannah Ellahi
West Midlands, UK

Simple Things

Ding-Ding Ding
Teachers stuffing children into classrooms like herds of sheep
Fiddling fingers
Quiet contemplation of whether to answer questions
Stomachs growling
Muffled giggling
Brains pounding
Craving a warm hearty dinner from Mom
Counting down in unison
3, 2, 1
Ding-Ding Ding
And the cycle repeats

Ding-Ding Ding
Teachers stuffing children into classrooms like herds of sheep
Fiddling fingers
Quiet contemplation of whether to answer questions
Stomachs growling
Muffled giggling
Brains pounding
Craving a warm hearty dinner from Mom
Counting down in unison
3, 2, 1
Ding-Ding Ding
And the cycle repeats

Ding-Ding Ding
Teachers stuffing children into classrooms like herds of sheep
Fiddling fingers
Quiet contemplation of whether to answer questions

Stomachs growling
Muffled giggling
Brains pounding
Craving a warm hearty dinner from Mom
Counting down in unison
3, 2, 1
Ding-Ding Ding
Yet this time the cycle abruptly stops
And never begins again

I miss the simple things
The simple things that made each day worthwhile

Hannah Ellahi aged 15 and is a student from the West Midlands in England. About the work: I created this short poem about how corona affected me. I was one of many pupils who had all my exams canceled, ones I had been preparing for almost five years. I wrote about the simple things that I encountered every day at school that I wasn't ready to let go of yet, but was forced to because of Corona. My last day of the school occurred without me even realizing due to the safety measures the UK had to put in place to keep us all safe. Simple things that corona snatched from our tight grasp.

Angus Emeka
Nigeria

One Day

Morning!
The sun is up,
So is the world.
Swift movements and giant strides,
Short pleasantries and forced smiles,
The rush hour like a raging tide,
The battle between man and time,
Money is the prize for this price.

Afternoon!
The sun still reigns,
Asserting rule by scorching rays,
Agility is mundanely displayed,
The battle is intensified,
Victor nor vanquished, time always flies,

One is disappointed, another satisfied,

Night!
The moon takes over,
The conquest is over,
Lonely streets and dark corners,
The family is back together.

Silence!
Hush world! A thief has entered.
This thief is a foreigner,
Traveling through borders without a visa,
From Asia to Europe to Africa.
Each creepy step is a disaster;

The world is bedridden;
Its health has been stolen,
All protocols are broken,

Its inhabitants are being taken,
Now your home is your haven,
Religion is praying,
Science is working,
Humanity is hoping.
Stay Home, stay safe!

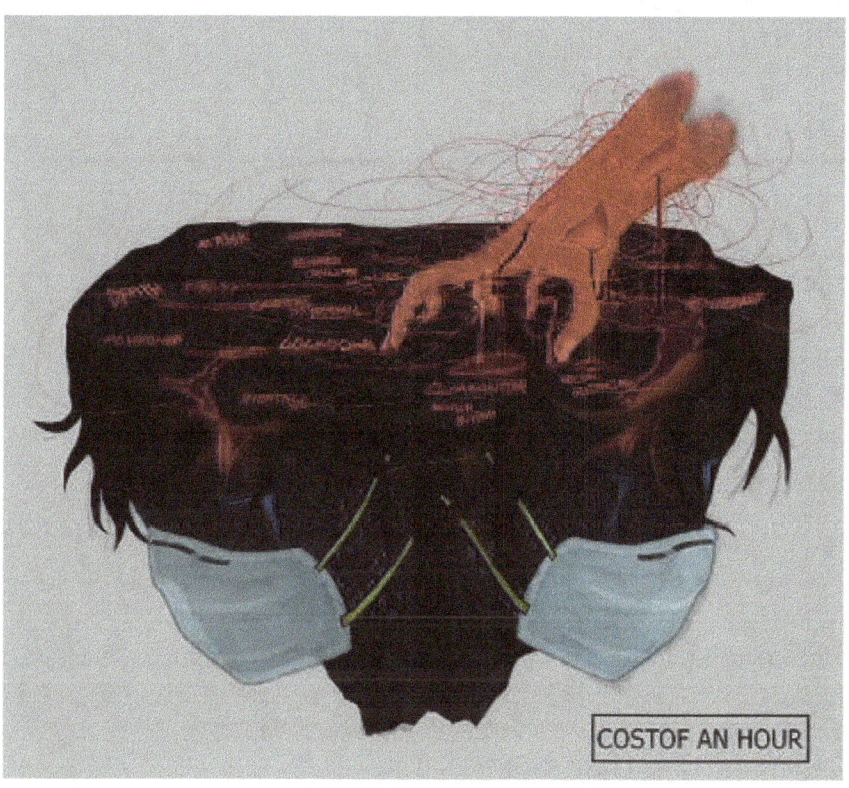

Cherie Fabular, Philippines. **Spread of Infection.** Cherie is a digital artist who studied at CIIT: College of Arts And Technology. The hand is the Coronavirus. The blood leaking from it is the infection. The threads surrounding the hand are the tension that are released from the hand, making the atmosphere of the area feel tense and eerie.

Adefemi Fagite
Nigeria

Swiftly It Came

Dark clouds capped the azure.
It was not the gathering of rain,
But an ominous threat of doom.

Earnestly it came,
The wind of death,
Swiftly and quickly billowing quiet venom

How do we appease you,
Agent of death?
What items of sacrifice do you require
Before you release the world from your deathly snag

First, you isolate your victim from their loved ones,
Then slowly, you take their breath away.

Alone in sickness,
Alone in death
Denied arrangement in their most elegant apparel,
They journey to the great beyond in a sanatorium frock.

Adefemi Fagite is an avid reader and author. His works have featured in several anthologies and magazines.

Agneta Falk /US

The Taste of Absence

We're at the window, the loud silence
of the water at a distance,
just lying there, undisturbed
but for a lone sailboat.

Across the alley, a house stands empty
torn apart by constructions,
waiting for the workers to return
to their abandoned tools.

Every day feels like Good Friday
prolonged by grief and birth pangs,
the birds chirpier than usual,
fluttering freely.

We're nurturing this silence, you making
marks on paper, I baking a cake
filled with apples, cardamom
and healthcare for all.
we're kicking Covid-19 out
of us by digging the deepest hole
for our deadly saliva to be
buried in forever.
The earth starts breathing again

*Agneta Falk is a Swedish/ American visual Artist, , poet
,,editor and translator.*

Fereidoun Farboud, Iran, art curator & photographer, founder and
manager of the Art for Peace festival

Shannon Gable
India

Corona the Pandemic

And just like that
The world goes silent,
And human civilization is homebound.

The air gets more precise and noise reduced
Vehicles seem to have halted,
And life came to a standstill.

Where the birds chirping hid behind
All the mess of living race,
And the chaotic buzzing has tremendously withered,
Off the passing days.

Disputes have forgotten, and differences kept aside,
Those Fighting each other are now standing beside
To find a remedy to completely eradicate,
And restore the dying human race.

Quarantined, Locked Down & Barred them all
Measures are taken to prevent its spread;
Stay Home, Stay Safe & wash your hands
Precautionary measures in our heads fed.

It will be gone soon enough
To one day be remembered as a lesson for all,
Let's take the steps necessary now
Before nations and humanity tend to fall.

This is just a setback we are facing,
Soon we will be back to life as we were living.

Plague 2020

A virus so small Has scared us all,
Amidst all this fear, We yet stand tall.

Finally, there will come the day again
The chaotic life we cannot refrain,
Living free and thriving then
A new way of living about to begin.

Stay Positive Stay Strong,
Let's face this setback once and for all;
Nevermore to see again
Such days where life is nothing but a living hell.

Mahaq Fatima, New Delhi, India

Jeremy Gadd
Australia

In A Time

In a time of deadly disease,
daily deaths, untold suffering,
plague pits in the USA and the
afflicted boarded up in their houses,
in Wuhan, so they say,
there might be a silver lining, now
rampant consumerism is denied:
cleaner rivers and tides, less polluted air,
animal shelters emptied by human
demand for companionship and despair;
reading Boccaccio's Decameron again;
enforced isolation strengthening family ties;
random acts of kindness being recognized.

Kishor Gaire / Nepal

Fearless Flying

Fearless flying in the open sky! I woke up very early today. My children were asleep, and I needed to gather food for us. I left the children alone in the nest to sleep and flew away in search of food before no one woke up. My Nest was a little far away from human settlements because nowadays, we couldn't coexist with humans. I feel that the goodwill and virtue in humans for us seems like a zero these days. When I see people being so cruel, I think that the age of the demon has begun. My beloved companion, we used to call her "Gitri", who was shot by stones fired from a slingshot when we together were flying to collect food by a boy for pleasure. How can humans be so cruel to us? In severe pain, before her last breath, she was whispering my name "Titri". I was hopeless. I couldn't do anything instead of saving my own life. I left my friend to die and ran away. Am I selfish? Its a question to myself. I flew and hid in a tree far away from the incident. I was seeing her and silly humans pulled all her feathers, and they were having fun at the barbecue. By luck, they didn't kill me. If I was killed then who used to care for my young ones. Till today if I think of that moment, I am shocked. My husband went in search of food and didn't return back till today. I miss him so much. Struggling with enemies for growing children is tough work that my husband gave me and flew forever. I wished him to be back in our life. Oh God! if you are the creator, preserver, and destroyer of this world, then please listen to me, return my husband. Punish the humanoid demons who play with our lives for the fun of the moment. Finally, the village was seen. There is a lake near the village. There is plenty of food that we need around that lake. Last time when I was in this lake, my friend fish explained what kind of torture they are facing from humans. Sometimes they flow current in the water for fishing, or sometimes they poisoned water in the lake and end all life in the lake. That is why nowadays we do not want to go to the lake. A couple of days before, at that time, when we were sleeping in our nest, the tiger and Tigress were passing from there. They were talking about the incident in which their cub mistakenly went to the wheat field. Humans kidnapped him and sent him to the zoo for lifelong imprisonment. From that day, Tigress left to eat food. The tiger was trying to convince the tigress to overcome the complication over the situation. It's not a matter of little bravery to listen to tiger and tigress conversation at that mood they had. But I can understand, she is fearful but a loving mother. Only a mother knows the pain of separation with her child. I could understand better because I am a mother too. With a fearful heart, flying in search of food is tough. I suddenly noticed an Elephant playing on the ground. I remembered that day. O God, it is hard to save lives! My sleep was disrupted by the commotion in my nest. People were carrying elephant ivory with guns in their hands; I watched all these with eyes wide open. If a giant animal-like Elephant is not secure to live his life on his choice, then how can we be safe from humans? fact is that we are birds. Today there was something strange, no sounds, the sky was clear, the atmosphere was calm, even I could hear the flowing river. The village had started to come, but I couldn't see the smoke coming from the chimneys of Industries. That smoke is so bitter that sometimes I feel I will die inhaling that harmful gases produced. Most of the time, when I was near industry, I always felt that I was about to die. Our Forest was formerly near this village with dense, thick trees, but today, forest and human settlement are farther away. It always hurt me that I was made homeless with my children due to deforestation. At midnight smuggler starts chopping down the trees for their greed fulfillment and thousands of creatures are made homeless. When they know without the tree, we can't even breathe. A week ago, I met a charming deer near the river where we all go for drinking water. That deer was drinking water suddenly I saw that he was in suffocation. It was the plastic bag which he drank with water, and it stuck in the deer's throat. He died with suffocation. People have already reached the climax of indecency by garbage dumping in the river. I don't have an adjective to define humans as clever or fools. They think they are clever enough, so they established a drinking water supply agency from where they get safe drinking water. Humans are the pot of greed and selfishness. They compel us to drink poisonous water contaminated with harmful chemicals from factories, sewages, and garbage that they throw in water resources. I think they are a fool. Why don't they think that our existence and human existence are interrelated when we are finished, it will not take time to finish human existence. I am surprised that I was near human settlement why there is silence. As I knew humans are not silent creatures, they are disturbing creatures. When they visit our forest in the name of a picnic, they put on loudspeakers and shout and enjoy not only that with their unwanted blowing of the horn of their vehicles irritates us. But today I am so close to their dwelling place, but I couldn't hear a single sound. How is it possible? Where are those cruel little boys creating a terror of slingshot? I am surprised. Is today a political strike in Nepal? Where are people? It was the subject of investigation for me. So before gathering food for us, I decided to investigate the situation of humans. To know the real situation, I flew towards the square. When I reached the square, I heard a notice from municipality authority that the coronavirus is terrorizing human existence. Till today thousands of people are killed by this virus, and a hundred thousand were infected by it. People were in fear, so the government of Nepal has decided to lock down the country for some time. It was the reason why people were not outside. I didn't feel good after hearing all this. I was in a panic, but I couldn't do anything for them. I was hoping to God. So I went to Temple for praying. I prayed with God at the temple to end up a demon virus named Corona, which had developed into a world full of horror and fear to end human existence. Lord! No matter how much humankind oppresses us, without this human being, this planet has no value. So I asked God to help humans to defeat the horror of the coronavirus. After praying, I went to collect food for us, on the way, I saw the people locked up in their own homes and their eyes towards the sky. The humans made me remember my old friend parrot, in the name of keeping a pet, they used to lock up them in a cage. This corona is locking them like a parrot. I felt pity towards them and flew towards the lake to gather food for us. After gathering some food, I flew back towards my nest, wishing them good health, and that was what I could do for them because I am just a bird. And the flight towards my nest was fearless flying in an open sky.

I'am MINU ELIZABETH PHILIP pursuing BTECH civil engineering at MBCCET, Peermade, Kerala, India. I am an Indian citizen and a keralite. I am from Pathanamthitta a district in kerala.

©minu

Vineeta Gejji
India

Corona Times

It felt like yesterday
When people complained
No time to spend with family
Hanging on to the clock
Racing with time
Tired, no time to stand and stare
Coming back to designer homes
Only to sleep
Not only bread and salt to be brought to the table
But a substantial fare was needed
Rooms filled with clothes, shoes, bags, accessories
Holidays to exotic locations, gluttonous eating
No one questioned where we were heading?
It was taken as a sign of being alive
And leading a fabulous life
Nature was tired of providing
No end to man's need and greed
And yet man complained
She had reached her tether's end
And lashed out at humanity
Grudgingly she said
Take not only "quality time."
But quantity time too
Stay indoors and realize
The extent of your exploitation
For if you LIVE then
All that you had accumulated will have meaning

Kaushik Ghosh
Dehradun, India

Life Under Lockdown

Constrained have become movements.
Love, joy, happiness, and humanity seem to be limited.
Nah! Not humanity. Not yet!!
Things you took for granted,
Something you always wanted (And things you didn't)
- All seems not that obvious anymore.
Your 'bai', the milkman, that routine handshake with that
inconsiderable colleague of yours Neighbors, shopkeepers and
campus cynosure
All of them, I guess, have started making sense in your life.
And as you stay home, playing with your kids like never before,
You realize life is not meant for paying bills; it's more, much
more.
The hug that you were embraced in the other day,
Your weekly ritual, when you assemble to pray
When you ask whereabouts to your fellow men, know you have
started missing them and have started asking - when?
When O' Lord would this night end
And when would light bend
To make its way into our lives
Which all of a sudden has started appearing as a blight.
But I know there will be light
There will be bright again and a new dawn
When we'll wake up from our slumber of bane with a yawn
And will realize - it's morning once again.
Once again my children will be able to meet their friends in school,
And your septuagenarian father will sit with his mate, having their
pitchers full,
And once again, the neighboring parks will be bustling with
laughter and light.

One beautiful morning your maid will turn up again, and you'll realize how you missed her.
Not because you had a tough time without her during this time;
But for the fact that you'd have discovered back the human- dead asleep deep within- during this time.

Ghosh is a faculty member in the University of Petroleum and Energy Studies in Dehradun, India.

Rex Max Gomez
Angeles City, Philippines

Social Parasites

We build home machines to make our living easy
We create mobile contraptions for our transportation
We clear forest for our expanding population
We create concrete & iron boxes for our dwelling
We pollute rivers and seas for our unending waste
We dig holes for coal, precious gems, and oil for our luxury
We skin alive animals for our ornaments, boots, bags, and clothes
We destroy different species to satisfy our exotic food craving
We used animals for our gluten grass cultivation, security, and
war.
We used chemical agents to destroy the vast forest to deny our foes
of shelter
We used bombs, napalm, and atomic weapons to have a deterrent
among states
We burned millions of tons of crude oil to deny our human foes of
means of a source of income
We create biological weapons to kill or mutate our enemies
We ravage our self of chronic diseases by using industrial
preservatives
We slaughter animals because of human-made infections.
We human are not needed by nature as we are the destroyer of life
We are the social PARASITE of Mother Earth, just like a deadly
blight.

*Rex Max Gomez; Information Technology Teacher from Angeles
City, Philippines. Hobbies are Military History, Weapon Systems,
Poetry, Software Development, and playing string instruments.*

Steven Gray
USA

Corona

When you sink into a deep domestic meditation
which is plausible because you're out of work along with
half the workforce and it has been going on for months,
you wonder who is in control and how much longer it will
last. The occupants sequestered in their insulated
boxes, reading books about "the staggering collapse
of U.S. intelligence" concerning the coronavirus
as a heavy blanket settles on the continent
consisting of a quarantine that is unwarranted
according to some and others think it's warranted and no one

wants to die. You think about it while you're on the roof deck
with a bottle of wine, your forehead being pounded by
relentless moonlight and the full moon is a tranquilizer
when there is a lot to worry about, the disconcerting
parallels between a medical necessity
and an authoritarian lockdown where the citizens
are not allowed to get together, and their mouths are covered
like their voices have been censored and they have to walk
alone. You're staring into space, communing with the mountains
of the moon, another way of social distancing.

There were warnings and rehearsals which were soon denied
(like 9/11), sounding like "It can't happen here." And whether
or not it was deliberate it is another occasion
where the profiteering meets the mass psychology
of fascism. The confusing information is a camouflage,
you try to bring a constellation into focus,
the tectonic shifts occurring in the government
are throwing off a lot of people and a cloud of money

flies around like starlings with the homing signal of a
corporation. It requires our cooperation.

The overlord who occupies the White House said, "I'll be your
oversight" and fired the man in charge of oversight.
Our leaders have the insight of a bag of hammers, it was
bred out of them by the system, it is adding to a
sense of dread. It leaves you in an existential trance,
you sit at home and listen to the sirens which are headed
for the pier, the Bomb Squad setting up a tent, the vehicles
are black. Is it a drill? You hear the virus killed
you and a folk singer want to write a song:
"CORONA CORONA,
what are you doing here… I hope you're gone next year…."

*Steven Gray is a writer and musician who lives in San Francisco,
California*

Dipjyoti Gowala, *Assam State, India*

Vrinda Haldia, India. Haldia has exhibited works with artists from 25 countries. She is fascinated by Indian traditional arts such as puppets of Rajasthan. Her studio is called House of Kalakaar

Abderrahim Hamza Marrakech, Morocco. COVID Story. Hamza is
calligrapher, musician, performer and muralist with works on the
walls of the Ochre City

Sanjida Bhuiyan Haque

Lockdown Poetry, A Few Random Lines

In the maze of life,
I thought I am near the exit door
Never knew I would step into an abyss of hopelessness
Such a free fall, painless till now
Because the depths are more profound than despair itself
I suffer in anticipation of the unanticipated
It's like looking forward to the light at the end of a black hole
Is it the end or just an evolutionary sharp turn
Is it karma in fast forward mode
Pushing us to meet our maker who is recalling defect products
A species called human, He wants to factory reset!

Jack Hirschman
USA

The Sur Ivan O'Roc Arcane

1.

Should I…?
If I go there…?
What if someone who
has it touches me?

I'm 86, I've had
pneumonia, been in
hospital with C.O.P.D.
as well. Should I

go on? It's all over
everything—computers,
CNN, androids, smartphones
. You're 74

in a couple of weeks,
love, which is also
on its age-register.
Keep your natural

humor sharp; it's
important to laugh
at the unknown or
even with it.

This coronavirus
wants to destroy
the Planetariet

just as it was being

born. China's smote,
Italy smote, Japan,
South Korea, Iran,
the United States

smote as well as
any and everywhere
else. This virus's
crown of the

pantheon of dis-ease,
the constellation of
Being framed by the
concealed true lie

that's truly the bio-
logical truth of the
pandemic explosion
in the atomic

devastation of the
The nucleus of the eye.

2.

People are afraid
of breath, that they'll
inhale this hell or
exhale it on others.

Afraid of touching
lest they pass it along.
People are living as
un-screamed shrieks,

in the anguish of an

angst abated only
by opiated oblivion.
Sur Ivan O'Roc

I misheard, thinking
it was an Irishman
who'd picked up the
the virus in California,

instead of the title
of this Arcane in
reverse, that is,
Coronavirus,

because everything's
in reverse, postponed,
set back, from sports
events, Disneyland,

operas, Broadway
theaters, concerts.
Laughter's been
restricted, belly

laughter zoned to
a living room or
a kitchen table.
We're all at home

anxiously waiting
for it to end because
a cough can nail me
to it, or my breath

breathes and doesn't
know if my exhalation
carries the bug of
the bat or the snake,

and all those Russian
vodkas have failed.
I'm telling you from
my 86 years that

the whole world's
been 86'd from its
happiness, forced
to live as if, as if

a zero had arrived
at all the numbers
of the world's peoples.
But look, in Italy,

amid hundreds
dying in a single
day, people stand
on the balconies

of their apartments
and sing the songs
close to their hearts
to warm their hearts

and hopefully this
can be a contagion
of hope confronting
the disease,

and houses of song
be born all over the
world to be the best
vaccine there is: all

of us singing for real
The Internationale!

Bio: Jack Hirschman was born in New York City and grew up in the Bronx. A copyeditor with the Associated Press in New York as a young man, his earliest brush with fame came from a letter Ernest Hemingway wrote to him, published after Hemingway's death as "A Letter to a Young Writer." He is known for his radical engagement with both poetry and politics. He has been instrumental in the formation of the Union of Left Writers of San Francisco and the San Francisco Poets Brigade. He is the former poet laureate of San Francisco.

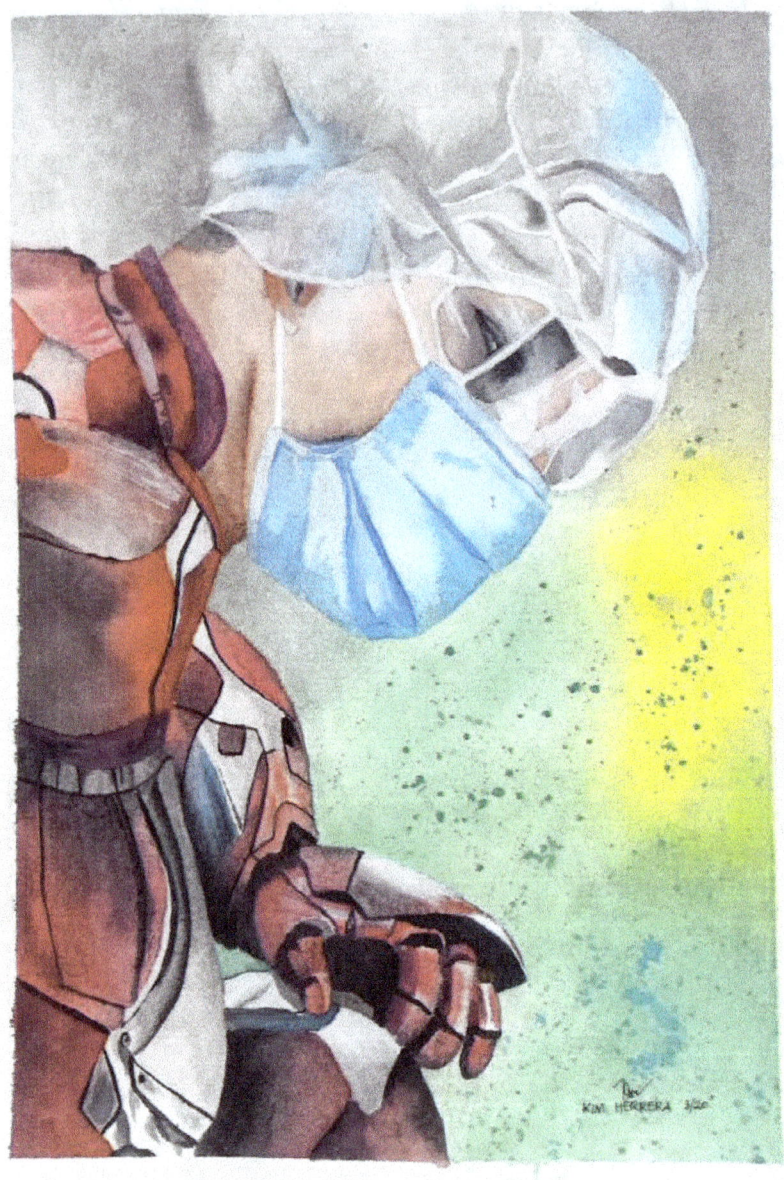

Remaur Herrera, Cebu, Philippines. Herrera is a 34-year old veterinarian and physician currently working as a general physician.

Ibrahim Honjo
Canada

They Play Hide and Seek, or
The Peekaboo Game

The land has opened its doors to the innocent
I breathe in the gentleness of death and sowing heavy sighs
I cannot ignore this boiling moment
In which the invisible riders of the apocalypse are sowing death
On the planet and take their tribute
To the luxuriant greed

Someone was spreading a virus around the Earth called the corona
It sprouts like mushrooms after rain on the planet
Rulers worried and perfidiously unskilled, they are going around in
circles
It is known in whose house the virus was born
And how it came into the world
It is not a product of evolution, nor is it a gift from God
It has a father and a mother, and it is conceived for a reason

Fear and silence are on the planet, and we are only talking about
the corona
It extinguishes all life, as slowly as a fire in a fireplace
Someone is secretly summing big profits somewhere
Hunger and poverty are knocking on our doors
We were slaves, and we will be even bigger ones
It seems to me, or I just may be dreaming

Do not fear my dear people, and do not sink into black thoughts
There is still hope for new awakenings and victories
This is just the game of invisible rulers
Standing with one foot deep into the grave

Everything is skillfully created, that man does not believe
anything
I wash my hands of everything and carry my burden
I wonder what is hiding behind the hill

Ibrahim Honjo is a Canadian poet /writer. Author of 30 published books in English and Serbo-Croatian language. Represented in more than 30 anthologies. His work has been published in many magazines. Some of his poems have been translated and published into Italian, Korean, Spanish, Mongolian, Slovenian, Polish, German, and Bahasa (Malesia) language. He received several awards for poetry.

Bakare Idris

Tell D next generation about Corona

A piece of words to the world
On a case that turns to a lord
Which sow the seed of fears in global eyes
That jeopardizes the world and agonize.

Let me tell it to the generation to come
How the world almost ends
How we keep dying one by one
How a virus nearly wipes the Nations as a whole.

Sending living souls below the soil
Causing emotional trauma and turmoil
Not even excepting a Chief of Staff
As Nigerians complain of the word "Starve."

I will tell the incoming generation
Of a disease that fears not the king,
Not to say of a serf.
Killing one and all, in the spotlight.

I will tell them the incoming generation.
What true wealth is!
That, it wasn't just a mere saying
That; HEALTH is WEALTH.

In case I survived,
I will tell the generation to come
How we are forced to self-isolations
And we are Compelled to social distances.

Plague 2020

Remember, nothing are we in the eyes of creator
In a fiction we are just an actor
That can be removed by director of play
By the actor, director ought to be obey.

Please remember to stay safe.

Mohammad Shafiqul Islam
Bangladesh

No One Weeps Anywhere on Earth Anymore

Silence has gripped the whole wide world
No one weeps anywhere on earth anymore
It seems everyone is waiting for the last call
The world is blanketed in despair and silence
The sky is looking strangely unfamiliar too
Sunshine doesn't arrive in the valley of deaths
People have forgotten to shed tears, to mourn
They're stunned at what's happening around
Rows of dead bodies are shutting off roads
Birds have joined the cortèges of silence
Bizarre breeze is blowing in off landscapes
Eerie creatures reign over the realm of humans
Ravaging city after city, enervating emotions
Fear in everything has put off the lights of life
Complacency and pride can't avert contagions
Because microbes live on, never die forever
Now human beings have their own decent jobs
That may keep them calm and Panglossian
But nothing ceases permanently from the universe
In a bright morn, birds will sing again soon

Mohammad Shafiqul Islam, the poetry editor of "Reckoning," is the author of two poetry collections, most recently "Inner State" (Daily Star Books, 2020), and translator of "Humayun Ahmed: Selected Short Stories and Aphorisms of Humayun Azad."

Dr. Garima Jain, *India. Stay Awa from Superstition—*

Sarthak Jain. *India*

Datu Nooh Jainal, *Philippines*. **Blood War**. Jainal is a preschool teacher focusing on painting and dancing. This art is a record of my thoughts. If only we had the superpowers of the fictional characters that we adore and have the ability to kill this pandemic ghost and recover what has been lost - our lives.

Warda Jamil, *Pakistan.* **None Can Save Us From Covid19 but ALLAH**

Noor Jellani

COVID-19

Shutdown the windows,
Close the doors,
The air you breathe in isn't pure anymore,
The hugs that you give,
Aren't safe more,
The handshakes of yours,
Transmits zillions of germs,
Wrecking my core.
Sshhh
Don't go out,
Or the police will bring u down to the floor
And beat you brutally,
Because you stepped out in the hell,
A place where once you use to walk,
A place where once you use to talk with your mates,
Is no safer,
Because a virus has taken over the planet earth,
And soon, all the things will come to an end.
A man around you has a power of cough,
With just one drop of germs, he can end your entity.
Be aware,
OH, humanity,
There's a killer a murderer in the town
Be safe
Be at home
Or end up on the death bed.
2020,
A year of change as expected,
Well, not every time things go around our expectations,
A cold war b/w indo-pak,

A world war between countries,
A country facing threats of Indians
A country who has no freedom
And on top of all these problems
Dear world,
Welcome Coronavirus,
A virus which has put half the world into disguise,
Or maybe it's a virus
Which connects all the humanity
And makes them stand united and
Find a way together
to put an end on the virus
Perhaps it's a way of world peace!
Whatever it is
It's a dangerous species
And we all must abide by the rules and precautions of medical staff
In order to stay safe.
This virus has led to so much
A human cannot walk around without a mask on
Face,
To filter all this infected air.
All the shops are closed, and a full lockdown has been set up,
Just to make sure the safety of people,
But what about the laborers?
What about the poor?
Who can't afford the corrupted society
Where a mask of 10 rs is being sold in 100rs
What about them?
What about their earnings?
Each solution is leading to many other issues
This whole drama is badly endangered.
Dear Corona
Leave our world.

Ashraful Kabir
Dhaka, Bangladesh

The Scent of Victory

Still the sun rises in the east
Still the sun sets in the west;
And still my heart longs for you.

Oh, April!
What do you have in your satchel?
You have come across a long way
With your scorching heat -
   To burn the greenish field
   To burn the fraternity
   To burn the planet
And eventually in this dire time
   To burn the dejected souls.
Don't you know?
   We forgot the lullaby
   We forgot the color of the fig tree; now
   We don't dare enjoy their beauty
We have been confined to a strange time!

Don't you know?
Tears and horrors are symmetrical nowadays,
It is the reign of pity and fear
The invisible Mephistopheles
   Has suppressed our feelings.
Yes, the climax is yet to come
But we don't want the climax again.

With due respect and proper submission,
We request you not to divulge any more surprise
   No more novelties

No more sighs
No more nuisances, please
Go back to your castle with the folded-satchel
'The sooner, the better'.

The west window is still closed
Can't open, for fear of the wind blowing
      I feel awful
Everyone says the war is not over yet
But I get that scent of victory.
The road is empty, the window is closed
Oh, the Omnipotent, please save us
We don't need this fearful world, having
      Any new nightmare imposed!

Kabir is an essayist, book reviewer & literary critic

Dora Kalinova, *Italy* Marina Novira *Beijing, China.* Novira is an Indonesian poet. Her book is Menyapa Rindu; *Hello, Longing.*

Shuvra Rani Kar

Bagladesh

Pandemic

A strange event in a small country suddenly caught all the attraction of international media all around the world. It all started just three months ago, and nobody ever imagined their lives could change in such a short time. It was the last day of July, 1st weekend after the lockdown was over. Though there was a heavy downpour on the last night, the sun was coaching since morning. Instead of having plenty of fish, meat, and vegetables at home, Mr. Badar, a government higher official, went to the fish market to buy some shrimps for his only 6 years old son. While returning by a rickshaw suddenly, that strange incident happened. Everyone, including the rickshaw puller, watched with strange eyes that Mr. Badar, who was just alright a moment ago, is now suddenly groaning on the floor like a jellyfish. His spine was no more there, but only a blue thin wire barely connected from his neck to his hip. Nobody had ever seen such a peculiar incident so as some got frightened some others started filming it. The incident happened just beside his house gate, so his wife and son rushed on the spot within a short time. They took him to one of the best hospitals but couldn't save him. He died in the ICU after 24 hours. Though it was a strange occurrence yet didn't get attention from many. It got lost among many other news of rape and murder. Some people watched the video of Mr. Badar groaning as a jellyfish but thought it might be a hoax. And the whole incident could be lost in Oblivion if the next occurrence won't happen. Just after 17 days, one of the richest persons in the country, Mr. Shafiq, died in the same way. He was just back to the country with his family after spending 3 long months abroad. He was taking a shower in

his luxurious bathroom while listening to jazz music. Nobody knows exactly when it happened, but his body was rescued by breaking the lock after almost 3 hours. He was lying on the floor and his body looked like a jellyfish exactly how Mr. Badar looked like 17 days ago. After this the media was on fire. People blew a storm over the cup. Everybody was accusing everyone, but nobody could see the wood for the trees. Within just 2months and 11days 237 people died in the same way-businessmen, politicians, religious leaders, celebrities and who not! And gradually people became more aggressive and scared. At last to find out the mystery behind the strange deaths, the prime minister formed a special secret team with all the higher intelligence officers, and scientists and doctors. The health minister, Mr. Nazim was appointed as the moderator and was ordered to report directly to the Prime minister. After 2 weeks, while having the evening tea, Mr. Nazim got a call from Mr. Mahmud, the chief coordinator of that special secret team, who had to report Mr. Nazim about their work progress. Having Mr. Nazim's approval, Mr. Mahmud appeared at his home within the shortest possible time. When Mr. Mahmud explained everything to Mr. Nazim, he couldn't believe his own ears. Is it really possible? Mr. Mahmud explained how all those deaths are related to the inhumane activities during the last global pandemic situation.
- First, Mr. Badar, during the pandemic, he stocked foods much more than he needed. Despite having enough money, he didn't help his poor neighbors either. Even his wife faced domestic violence during the lockdown. Second, Mr. Shafiq was a billionaire and was the owner of 27 garments. He put pressure on the government to keep the garments open during the lockdown for his profit. He didn't take into consideration the health issues of the workers. Even he didn't pay their salaries timely though he had billions. All the other cases had the same connection. The people who didn't obey the lockdown and risked other's lives, people who stocked foods except caring the poor neighbors, people who stole the relief goods, people who mistreated or misinformed the doctors, all are included in the list who died in the same way.

112

That pandemic was a revenge of nature to us. It required us to be more human. But some of us showed inhumane behaviors during the crisis. It's another revenge of nature to those who didn't keep their backbone strong enough not to bow down in front of greed and anger and lies. And I'm sorry to say sir, but your name is also on the list who are going to die like this. - Me!!! Mr. Nazim exclaimed - Yes sir, you have been the health minister, but you didn't perform your duties rightfully. Our doctors didn't get enough PPE on time during the pandemic; you didn't take enough care of their requirements. Mr. Nazim knew; all those accusations were true. As Mr. Mahmud left, Mr. Nazim became restless. He couldn't sleep the whole night. He remembered all his wicked acts just for a luxurious life, and these all seemed to him like trash. As the dawn started to appear, Mr. Nazim took out his revolver from the drawer and pointed to his own head. Precisely at the same moment, he felt a strange tingling on his backbone.

Arundhati Kalyan, Abundance: Covid-19

Nelson Kamkuimo
Cameroon

The Despot

No prince even in his most glorious days
ever succeeded in conquering the earth
moreover, in such a short period of time

yet we are today under the yoke of a fierce despot
who rose from a private station a few months ago
and has already turned mankind
into a pack of dogs subjected to his foolish rules

he instills fear in our hearts; he tortures our body our mind
and more than any natural disaster
his short-term reign has already made an alarming death toll

added to the world's agenda by chance he has ended up taking its
control
pushing our occupations back to the frontiers
he has ordered to build invisible barriers between our beloved ones
and us

*Nelson Kamkuimo is a Cameroonian poet, short story writer,
literary translator, and English Language teacher. He has published
in a dozen anthologies and literary magazines across the world.*

Kriti Kapoor
Delhi India

Here It Goes...

Trapped inside our homes.
Caged inside our rooms.
The chains & the shackles though invisible.
But our fates are left in the hands of the invincible.
Who would have thought, a day like this would come?
When life will be on a standstill, and feelings will go numb.
I miss the sky, I miss the sun,
I miss my friends, I miss the fun.
My heart feels sad, my anxiety knows no bound,
Seeing all the news, my thoughts roam around.
What have we done to our mother nature?
How could we have become such traitors?
We take and take and take and take.
Not pausing for a minute to take a break.
And, she knows what it's like to see her children fight,
Her heart pains to see the world in a constant riot.
So, maybe she has rightfully put us in our place.
Maybe it's time to slow down the pace.
The fear is real and so were our cruelties.
And, so was the nature of all of our dualities.
This is the time to make amends.
To stop being her enemies, and start being her friends.
Nature knows well enough all the math.
It's time to bring down the worldwide negativity and wrath.
We are being given a reboot button to set the records straight.
So, don't you let this all go to waste.
The world is already seeing miracles, the change has already
begun.
Let's stay indoors and let nature take its turn.
Hoping we can pick it up from where we left.

Correcting our actions and rebuilding our broken nest.
We'll soon get to see another sun.
We'll soon get to feel the airbrushing on our face when we'll start to run.
Till then let's cleanse what's been rotting inside.
Let's for once be the children our mother can look at with pride.

Kriti is an artist, loves writing, traveling, & food. She is currently on a self-healing journey. The sun, the moon & the clouds are my friends. She says, "I'm on a mission to make every person and place more joyful."

Nilanjana Kar/ Kolkata, India

CoronaVirus - Boon and Bane

Men enjoyed the slaughter of nature;
asserted supremacy all too much
from devastating their families
to making them homeless;
they delighted all.

But just then the crouching virus
jumped in, a savior for some,
an annihilator for others.
He was overthrowing the natural ways of being.
While humans and industries
were behind lock and key
faunas uncaged, floras bloomed
the wind sweetened and the sky purified.

Fathers & brothers & sisters & wives
gave themselves to Mother Earth;
prayers remained unheard,
havocs continued & households were ruined.
Kids lost their childhood,
lovers old age, elder's last wishes.
Roads got deserted & homes blackened
only frequent sobs and sirens heard.
Tears got exhausted slowly;
death not feared anymore, but awaited.
Yet amidst this, in unknown alleys,
some thanked divinity,
for the restoration of equality.

Nilanjana Kar hailing from West Bengal (Kolkata) situated in India.
Kar likes writing, reading, listening to music, cooking.

Arudchelvam Kartheheyen
Sri Lanka

What I Find

Locked in my room,
I look outside
A barren ghostland
It is what I find.

From the never closing' bars
To the ever buzzing' bazaars
All have fallen in slumber,
Leavin' us all in deep somber

Cramped up in isolation,
Haven't seen my friends in days
The sheer pain of separation
Is breaking me in many ways

So lonely and so quiet,
Yet my mind is in a riot
Can't even enjoy a slice of meat,
Knowing that murderers roam the streets

So, I switch on the TV
To ease my mind,
Perhaps a little movie
Would do just fine,
But, the news: 'Corona's Killing Spree.'
Is what I find

Arudchelvam Kartheheyen is a Grade-12 student

Apar Sharma Kaushik New Delhi, India. **"SHE WAS BURNING"**
This sketch is to portray the situation of Mother Nature in the recent past,
we the humans, almost destroyed her life, made her feel like hell, she
was burning with the outcomes of all the harmful acts that we chose
against her, and thus she was giving birth to a harmful Virus to take her
revenge, she was full of rage and anger, and present situation on the earth
is the result, how she burst out on us

120

Hira Kazmi

Fatima Khalid *Karachi, Pakistan*. **The Golden Book of Life**.
Creation of Adam brought suffering to humankind, we know that we
share only one religion that is humanity, and this crisis is bringing
humanity out of people. Tea wash and gouache on wasli paper.

Mahir Ali Khan
Malaysia

Under the Mahogany Tree

Under the Mahogany tree
Where it smelled of sweet timber
My head crawled up like a stranger
To the sound of birds

And up in the canopy
Where the light sprayed into me through the leaves
My absence was the god
My sound was the birds

Paniz B Khan

United Kingdom

Coronavirus Acrostic

Could get worse
Or get better
Really want this to change
Overnight nobody has left their house
Not all people are wearing masks
All the grocery stores have lines now

Very bad virus like this one are making people die
I'm also very happy that the schools are closed
Right now we have our mom teaching us
Uncle is calling us a lot
Saviz learned a brontosaurus poem during coronavirus break

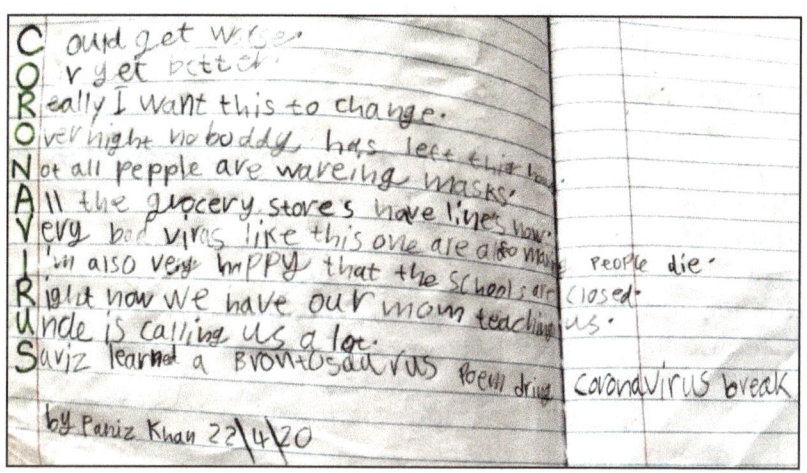

C ould get worse.
O r yet better.
R eally I want this to change.
O ver night no boddy has left that house.
N ot all pepple are wareing masks.
A ll the grocery stores have lines now.
V ery bad virus like this one are also making people die.
I m also very happy that the schools are closed.
R ight now we have our mom teaching us.
U ncle is calling us a lot.
S aviz learned a Brontosaurus poem during coronavirus break

by Paniz Khan 22/4/20

Paniz B. Khan *is a 7-year-old girl living in the UK*

Iffat Mahmuda Khan

EVANESCENT

I never knew how much patience
I have until this chapter
You know, my love?
The touch we once shared is now gone
The laughter has muted days back
We have lost all our inseparability
You are not anywhere near me.
But how,
How I'm going to tell you about the sky, trees, ocean. Can you hear me from
the ground?
Do you know?? The dead sky is living now...
Let me tell you about the trees, my love,
How scared they were of us?

Now, they are growing, dancing with the wind
And the ocean... oh mighty ocean....
She is laughing with her translucent beauty Love, is it too much to ask?
To live humbly, just to live with each other
Surely, I'll walk again, I'll dive, cry,
laugh, and I'll play with joy
But this time I would do it carefully,
I'd do it with all of them.

Again, I'll dive, cry, laugh, and I'll play with joy, but this time I would do it
carefully, I'd do it with all of them.

Saviz B. Khan *United Kingdom. Girl With Coronavirus Coughing. Saviz is Paniz's little sister. She is 5 years old.*

Shazly Khan *Pakistan*. Hoping and Praying for Paradise on Earth

Seigunlien Khongsai
Mumbai, India

This Too Shall Pass

As the world standstills amid adversity
Reflect for a moment to see the possibilities
As the fast pace race came to a halt
The fast pace mind began to instill quietness

It all started with an outbreak
And had given us all a break
What we all have thought as an epidemic
Infer us with the news of the pandemic

Is it nature's way of retribution
Or punishment for our lack of contribution
We all feel dismayed with the situation
Yet can't help but comply with the Isolation

Take this time to cherish each moment
But not costing the less privilege to resentment
Working together to assuage our fear
Helping each other to erase our tear

Indulge ourselves with the beauty of serenity
Refrain ourselves from the surge of anxiety
Ascertain that this will not last
Believing that this too shall pass.

Hailing from Manipur, India, Seigunlien is fascinated with the quote
"Live and let live" as he believes humanity comes before everything.

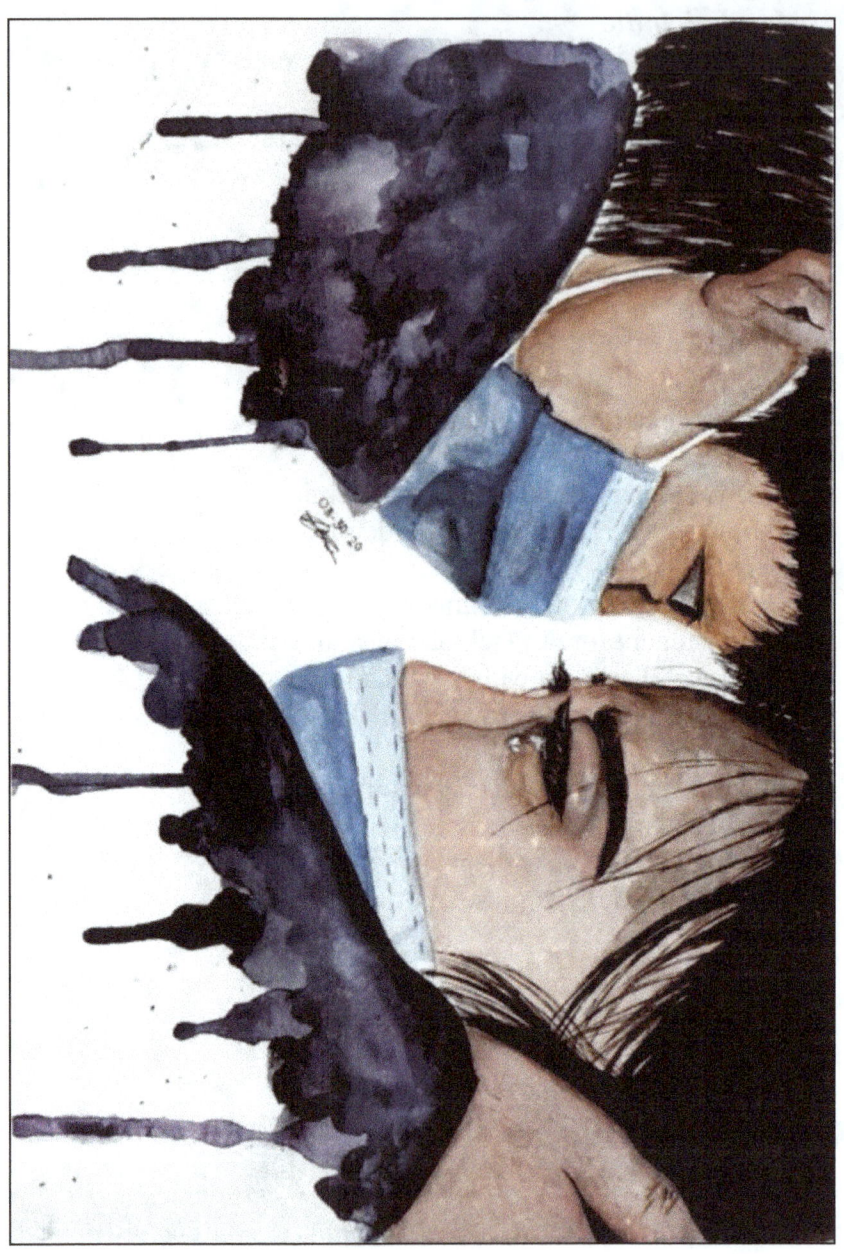

Aizell Lacuesta *Saskatchewan*, *Canada*. **Strength**. A couple from Wuhan, China fears the threat ofHammad Taufiq **Covid-19**

Richard Legaspi Philippines

Making Love with the Wind in the Time of Pandemic

(A farewell poem)

The memories of a journey constitute a prayer
And a never-ending quest is a pledge.
Never-ending, endless
It seems like it's leading to nowhere
If you can print the whisper of the wind,
Maybe it is one infinite poem.
If the dews are your tears,
Continue to wet the weed-like me.

If disappearing is as easy as covering the mountain with clouds,
And as poetic as drowning
Slowly help me disappear, drown me.
The memories of a journey
Don't end with a farewell,
They pile up with the wind
From the sighs that can only be heard at night
I repeatedly capture. I frequently hide.

The clouds are eternal witnesses,
You cannot hide the dawn
Until I haven't cried out this precious feeling
I will fly and fly until you notice me.
But if not, I will return, and I will gaze at your beauty.
Since you can't embrace my wholeness as you desire.
Goodbye, but how?

Richard Soriano Legaspi is an artist, writer, and filmmaker. He was a UNESCO-Aschberg Bursaries recipient in 2013 and Asian Film Academy, fellow.

Martin H. Levinson
USA

Covid-19

Bad news wrapped in a protein/
acellular saboteur/ a biological
Chernobyl exploding in a
leaderless land/ triage tents/
portable morgues/ white latex
gloves on a city street/ the virus
kills / it screams you must change
your life/ Zoom consoles but
touch is above technology/
no one wants to die alone/ a
doctor cries "we need more
beds, protective gear, there's
no way out but through."

Martin H. Levinson is a member of the Authors Guild, National Book Critics Circle, PEN America; the book review editor for ETC: A Review of General Semantics, and a contributing editor to The Satirist. He has published nine books and numerous articles and poems.

Annie Lledo
Philippines

COVID-19 Characters

In the morning the ants busy
Themselves with every grain they see
Two ants work very eagerly
One ant maintains the grain's safety
Last ant is ranting and angry
In the noontime the ants busy
Themselves with each grain to carry
Two ants work so efficiently
One ant maintains the grain's safety
Last ant is ranting and angry
In the evening the ants busy
Themselves to end the tiring day
Two ants work very orderly
One ant maintains the grain's safety
Last ant is ranting and angry
The ants are done, rest finally
The food arranged is now ready
Two ants turn up eat happily
One ant maintains the grain's safety
Last ant is ranting and hungry

Annie Velasco Lledo worked as a field reporter and newscaster but discovered joy in teaching language and literature. She is from the Philippines.

Jessica Loos
USA

Night Before the Night Before

It's the night before the night before
& l take another sip before the last sip
before the SIP starts, & Alan Black takes an eerie spec at the end
& l go home.

I sip some more last sips before the SIP starts for real, enact social
distancing, & have half a chicken for three Washington & a glass
of wine at Bella Cora.

March 17 l go out. SIP day 1. Sip 3,000.
The North Beach streets are vacant & heavy; my body cuts thru the
air, is there air?

A shrill-voiced woman in a pink bandana runs up behind people
walking, screams "boo" into their ears, sticks her tongue out, runs
away.

An older man with a cane & a brown paper bag throws a can at
her, spits on the sidewalk, asks me for a cigarette, screams at the
sky.

A guy with a mouth of silver caps leans against the wall on
Columbus, next to the taco place, blaring his radio & singing " We
Are The Champions," by Queen.

I go to my airless room & prepare for what? Sip 3,001. If only l
could see things outside instead of just into the fuckin' air well.
Just a tree, or a lunatic.

March 18. SIP day 2. On my way to Washington Square Park. People don't look as shell shocked. The sun's barely out. It's windy as fuck.

A young girl in all black, tattoos, a nose ring, boots & a dog strolls by, balancing a crate of eggs burning incense, singing "Good ship Lollipop."

Next, maybe I'll see the guy who walks his duck on a leash in a green jacket or the woman who never has any pants at all. Tomorrow is just day 3.

Jessica is a poet and activist from San Francisco, CA

Mario C Lucero

Not All Heroes Wear Capes

I wish to become a Superman,
and fly across the land
Catch people when they fall,
In the destruction of planet Krypton.
Everything is in control
balancing your body and soul
Man of steel, no one can steal
the power soon I will reveal!

I wish to become like Batman
and go straight to Wuhan,
Tell them to stop eating animal
like pangolins and the bats,
Respect the lives of these creations
or else we suffer from their wraths,
Of spreading a deadly virus
which will make the world collapse!
I wish to become like Aqua man
and talk to the Queen of Atlantis
Feel the current of waters
as I go down the deep,
Penetrate the Pearl of the Orient
and have promises to keep
That man suffers the consequence
of one's action in convergence!

I wish to become like Spider-Man
and swing with a silver web
Escape from this reality

stay in a safe and peaceful abode,
I will bring you to planet Mars
start a new life and count the stars
Forget all about the sufferings
and enjoy a new beginning!

I wish to become like Iron Man
and lead our government
Protect the people from corruption
equality must be felt,
Serve the community with passion
fair, just and humane
We only pass through this world once
and will never live gain!

Being like those superheroes
Is everybody's wish
Just stay at home
and you can save more lives,
Today is the time to give
and never become selfish
Because not all heroes wear capes
they are at home, you must believe!

Nicomedes S. Lumontad
Philippines

The Pestilence

Chaos brought by the virus has dominated the world stage.
Optimism and options to contain it are lacking and frustrating.
Responses have been put in place, though.
Ordering and using masks are the new normal.
Novel coronavirus spells havoc to humanity,

Annihilation or rehabilitation of this planet, that's the contention.
Virulent disease never ceases humanity's compassion.
Initiatives to protect and be protected are game-changers.

Reviving Mother Nature and practicing basic hygiene become
intensified human routines.

Understanding humanity amidst this crisis is beyond common
sense.
Showcasing deeply-felt kindness is more potent than cures and
vaccines.

Manohar Luthra/ New Delhi, India

Our Perception and Deception

Our perception was we can save the earth
It was a deception; earth can heal itself on its own
Our perception was we can't live without junk food
It was a deception; we eat healthy food at home
Our perception was we all need to go to the office to work
It was a deception; some of us can work from home
Our perception was we alone own this planet
It was a deception; animals have equal right for space on this earth
Our perception was oil is priceless
It was a deception; oil has no value without us
Our perception was we need to go on vacation to rejuvenate
ourselves
It was a deception; we can rejuvenate ourselves at home by doing
meditation and pursuing our hobby
Our perception was Americans and Europeans are more intelligent
It was a deception; more people are dying in the developed world
than in the underdeveloped world
Our perception was we can't do without shopping malls
It was a deception; our needs are limited, we need less to survive
Our perception was movie stars are real heroes
It was a deception; the real heroes are doctors, their staff, police
and social workers
Our perception was wrong; the world is still moving with minimal
human intervention
Cows give milk; hens lay eggs, air and water are cleaners, flowers
still bloom
Artificial life has ceased to exist
Real-life is not affected, it persists

*Manohar Luthra is a poet with a Post Graduate in English
Literature.*

Karen Melander Magoon
San Francisco, USA

Old Wisdom

We speak in many languages
As nature talks
In the speech of the wind
And raging oceans
The light of the sun
The scent of roses
The crush of snow
And crystals of ice
Our speech floats in the air
Conveying only what is received
Layered in dissonance or harmony
Over words or thoughts
Jangled untidily among us
The moon
Asks us to observe
Floating space
Her craters and valleys
Say little
Cradled in silence
Drifting above
River cascades below
Tumble and carve
Valleys and mountains
Throwing rocks
The mallet of Michaelangelo
Discovers artistry
Hidden in secret caverns of Gaia
Great spirits embrace old wisdom
While we layer animus over animus
Forgetting to be still

And listen to our hearts
Beating quietly among tangled debris
Pounding gently through conflicts
Sinking into the earth with homo naledi
The precursor of compassionate Neanderthal
Arms outstretched
Yet layered again with the war
Or simple quarrels
Spoken in many languages
Yearning to break free
To sculpt a new world
With old wisdom

Karen M. Magoon is a poet, pianist, and songwriter.

Devorah Major
San Francisco, USA

Covid-19 and the Homeless

i wonder at those
in doorways
under canvas tents
sheltered beneath cardboard cartons
inside dented cramped cars
their dry coughs echoing
into the night as they shiver
inside their fevered flesh
what does pandemic mean
to the homeless who
we have already
socially distanced
easily averting our gaze
righteously avoiding
getting close enough
to put a dollar into a palm
a smile into shadowed eyes
not seeing
much less acknowledging
that they have lived for years
in a pandemic
of poverty a pandemic of hunger
a pandemic, of danger
a pandemic of struggle
with minimal reward
what now of this new virus
pushed down their burning throats
to rest inside their eternally broken hearts
what now

*Devorah Major served as San Francisco's Third Poet Laureate
(2002-2006).*

Abdullah Al Mamun

Incoherent Thoughts

No touch, no hug,
Not even coming too close,
A sense of disbelief and fear
Surrounds the air,
None to believe,
None to share or admire
A sense of disbelief and fear
Surrounds the air.

Wearing mask and washing hands,
Keeping distance from social band,
Imitating Lady Macbeth in mind
Trying to hide the tension going wild.

The world is engulfed with terror
Time to reflect on self-mirror
The vain attempts we made
Denying all ethics and moral trade

We tried shining with material end.
Brought us nothing but empty den.

Carlito Manga
Philippines

Unredeemable

Time flowed like cement. He checked the wall clock hanging beside his mother's oak wood drawer. A minute had passed since he last checked, or so it seemed. Sitting there with nothing to stare at but a wall with chipped cream paint was excruciatingly dull. It was so pointless too. He decided to enter his mom's room and sit beside her deathbed. She's been home quarantined for days now. Being positive with the virus made her skin pale, eyes tired, and body weakened. Seeing his mom barely breathing while her eyes were tightly shut, tormented him, making his tears fall apart. The blanket covering her should've been filled with tears now.

He stood and walked out, knowing that he can't handle the pain of watching his mother in agony. He wandered around their house while thinking about how lucky he is. It's not because he's immune or fortunate to be dodging the disease, it's because he can't be infected from the first place. He died four years ago because of something more incurable., Cancer. Now he's just a soul guiding the one who gave birth to him.

Wiping his tears away, he whispered, "You'll be seeing me again any moment now, mom."

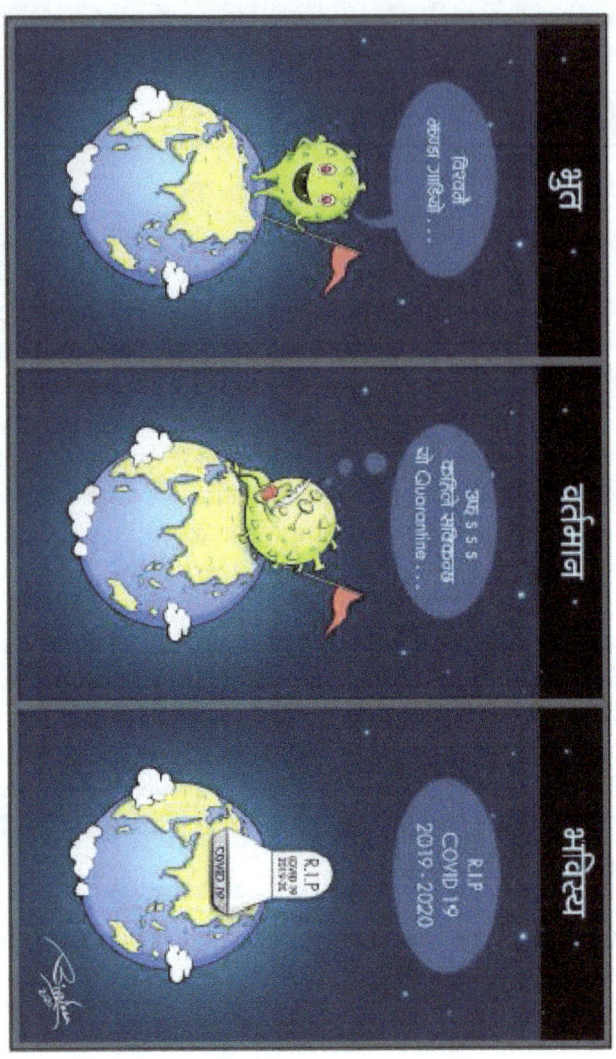

Birochan Malla *Kathmandu, Nepal.* About the work: In this illustration the past present and future of coronavirus are shown. On the first (past) panel corona's dialogue: we concord the whole world. On the second (present) panel Corona's dialogue : grrrr when will this Quarantine end ... ? On the third (future) panel (RIP covid 19).... I'm assuming within 2020 the virus will be wiped out.

Rosemary Manno
San Francisco, USA

Black Spring Again

Step outside to die
then come home if you have one
Detroit bus driver dies of the plague
citizens of streets and prisons
all front line workers in the human chain of disease
another episode in life and death
never one without the other
never make the same mistake twice

the flames
the floods
disasters still unnamed
we are almost equal in this crapshoot game

the face of democracy
death mask of a ravaged planet
suicides presage the end
vanguard of lockdown
an infected world awaits the unknown

Tree of unknown fruit blossoms in black spring
interspecies bonding with the pigeons
a roadside shrine remembers

All hail to thee
will we ever meet again?
the mystery is stronger than any love

When will I see you again?
all that can happen between now and then

so much already that makes tomorrow a first dream
on the horizon of a new time zone

Turn the wandering Jew around
all leaves flourish in the sun
stronger stems placed in the dark side now
to level the field of life
in a community of soil

You're a carrier
stay away
there's too much street in your environment
years and years of urban living have made you this way
it was always in the country where we became dirty

Cold mornings awaken to a fearless course
to never surrender before the battle is over
before the end of a siege
before the enemy captures
a time without time
a new place
the great unknown
to go home without you

Manno's collection "Marseille" was published in April 2019. She has authored many chapbooks and is also a visual artist.

Mayank Mehta
Kanpur (Uttar Pradesh) India.

Where the War Was Fought

जंग लड़ते थे देश की सीमा पर,
आज देश ही जंग का मैदान है।
कहाँ छिपा है, कहाँ बैठा है
ये डर भी कितना नादान है।।

दो वक्त की रोटी थी सपना जिनका,
उनका ना अब कोई ठिकाना है।
पहले मुसाफिर मंजिल के थे ,
अब मकसद बस जान बचाना है ।।

क्या गरीब क्या अमीर;
 दोनों को ही लड़ना है,
एक को सिर्फ बिमारी से,
तो दूसरे को भूख से भी मरना है।।

न आएंगे राम, न अल्लाह,
और ना ही आएंगें गौतम बुद्ध
अब तो जागो ओ देशवासियों,
 ये नहीं है कोई धर्म का युद्ध।

मौत का कोई आरक्षण नहीं
तो हमने क्यों भेदभाव किया,

पहले धरती लाल धर्म से
अब धरती ने खुद रक्त पिया।

अब तो जागो सोने वालों,
किसका भगवान बचाएगा।
इंसानियत से बढ़कर कुछ नहीं,
ये कौन तुम्हे समझाएगा ।।

नाप चुके हैं धरती अम्बर,
खुली हवा में भी अब ना निकला जाए
कैसी ये घड़ी देखो आन पड़ी,
जैसे बाहर खड़ा हो रावन;
और माँ सीता लक्ष्मण रेखा पार खड़ीं।।

परमाणू शक्ति से धमकाया सबको,
चाँद पर परचम लहराया था।
किसी काम का विज्ञान नहीं अब,
जिससे इंसान का पुतला तक बनाया था।।

विफल हुआ विज्ञान,
अदृश्य हुआ भगवान,
शायद ही कोई रास्ता होगा,
ढूंढ उसे नादान,
ढूंढ उसे इंसान।
ढूंढ उसे इंसान।।

The war was fought on the borders of the country,
Today the country is a battleground.
Where is it hiding, where is it sitting
how innocent this fear is.

He whose dream was to earn the bread of two times,
Now he has no whereabouts.
Earlier he was a traveler for destinations
Now his only target is to save his own life.

Whether rich or poor;
Both have to fight,
One only from illness,
while the other has to die of hunger too.

Neither Ram nor Allah
Nor will Gautam buddha come
Now wake up, O countrymen,
This is not a war of religion.

There are no reservations in death
So why did we discriminate,
Earlier the earth had been made red with religion
Now the earth itself is drinking blood.

Now wake up you sleepy heads,
Whose God will save us now
Nothing is greater than humanity,
Who will explain to you now

Those who had already measured the earth and sky,
Now they can't even come out in the open air
Look, what time has come
Like Ravan standing outside;
And Sita across the Laxman Rekha.

Threatened everyone with nuclear power,
even waved the flag on the moon.

but science is of no use anymore,
Which was even used to make man's clone.

Science has failed
God has become invisible
There is hardly any way now
Find it ignorant
Find it, man
Find it.

Mayank Mehta works in the Merchant Navy and is also an entrepreneur. He has a flair for poetry, loves to travel, and enjoys a humanitarian approach to life.

Gabriella Miotto/US

Love in the Time of COVID-19

Now that you are not allowed to touch me
I want to be sheltered by the language of the birds
and a thundering Buffalo drum
heart of one who returned from near-extinction.
I want to be sheltered by the language of the birds
while il medico della peste wears an N95 this time around
and the heart of one who returned from near-extinction
watches us make green pesto and music for one another

while il medico della peste wears an N95 this time
not smelling of lavender and mint but memento mori still,
and watches us make green pesto and music for one another
even though potato bins are empty and paper hoarded

not smelling of lavender and mint but still memento mori
we rage instead at death, block the reaper's entrance
even though potato bins are empty and paper hoarded
and dolphins return to Molo Audace and skies reclaim their blue

and we laugh at death, block the reaper's entrance
hear a thundering Buffalo drum
as dolphins return to Molo Audace and skies reclaim their blue
now that I am not allowed to touch you.

Gabriella Mariafiore Miotto is a family physician of Italian-American ancestry who has worked in community medicine in California, Alaska, Mexico, Guatemala, and the Balkans.

Prathamesh Mishra
Mumbai, India

No Homo Sapiens

No homo-sapiens on the goddamn roads,
No sweaty people carrying tonnes of worldly loads,
No technical machine chaos around
No rape, no violence, and no irritating sound.

Flying free for the first time in history
Dogs were unsolving, no human mystery.
Heard birds' & crickets chirping after long
Bright flowers untouched & rituals went wrong,

All dangerous human Lions in the den
Trees giving no timber but only oxygen,
Good, they aren't going for Quarantine,
It seems that human nonexistence is all fine!

For a change, no caste, no sect, no creed,
But how will they get rid of their vices and greed,
No discrimination still compulsory untouchability
Villages are flourishing, and deteriorating is the city.

People meeting their families for hours at a stretch,
Playing music, dancing with moms and curating a sketch,
No beer, no cigarettes, recreation, outdoor sports or Rum
A paradise for introverts but very difficult for some.

Viruses have no brains and just are doing this for survival,
Is it the end of Kaliyug and Mother Earth's Revival,
We aren't the cherry on the cake, but only a pinch of salt.
We are supposed to be the smartest,
But a nanoparticle brought everything to a halt!

Dede Montgomery
West Linn, OR, USA

Mourning

I miss her.

This mother of mine.

My missing her is different than that of Dad. He who already left this earth.

I'm an unknown shape to her through the window unless it's a good day. She sees the darkness in my hair—outline of my lips in a smile against the paleness of my skin.

My wave a confusing blur to these eyes no longer seeing clearly. My voice is garbled on a speaker.

I remind her—your daughter. your favorite. Only. You, my mother. My favorite. My only.

She smiles. Sometimes. On good days she laughs.

But if it is her daughter, why don't I come in and hug her? I remind her, and she nods her head. Slowly. In sad agreement.

I sing to her, and on good days she sings along. I go slowly so she can keep up. A delay between my phone and what I barely hear as the speaker echoes through the window. I sing another. She shakes her head and says no. Is it too sentimental? Good times than, not now? Suddenly she is disturbed. Songs like that don't belong in this weird world that none of us can understand, including her.

I read to her, selecting only funny or simple stories through this complicated communication. On good days she laughs, smiles, nods along. On bad days she closes her eyes. Asleep or elsewhere, I'm not sure.

My voice catches. No crying. I can't cry, not now. I need to be the strong one. I need to pretend: yes, all is well. Stop the tears now. Until later. After.

All I want to do is sit outside in the sun and hold her hand.

No words. Stare at the blue of the sky and the green of the first.

Peer out into this magical world, blurry for her, clear for me. Nature that is strangely still here. Wondrous and awakening in the spring with peachy tulips rimmed with yellow, laden catkins drooping from maples.

Yes, I say. We are lucky—some of the lucky ones. I don't feel lucky.

She has had a good life. A long one. She knows. But not now. Not as she had hoped it would be now.

Me too: family, children, a paying job and benefits, roof over my head, and food in the pantry. And yet I cry. More tears stream today than yesterday in this passage of time. After each window visit and telephone call and facetime.

Many more days than not I now hope she might pass peacefully one night. Soon.

But not soon if we can't see her?

Not too soon for her to laugh at grandsons and smile with her only daughter and granddaughters and sons with faces close enough to know. To smell and feel our love.

Not too soon to be out in the green and blue together again.

And yet. We're lucky. We are the fortunate ones—Tears drip. I grieve.

I miss her.

This mother of mine.

Dede Montgomery is the author of three books, including her memoir, My Music Man, by Bedazzled Ink Publishing. She works in occupational safety and health, and lives near Portland,

Anisha Mukherjee *India*

Indranil Mukheriee *Mumbai. India*

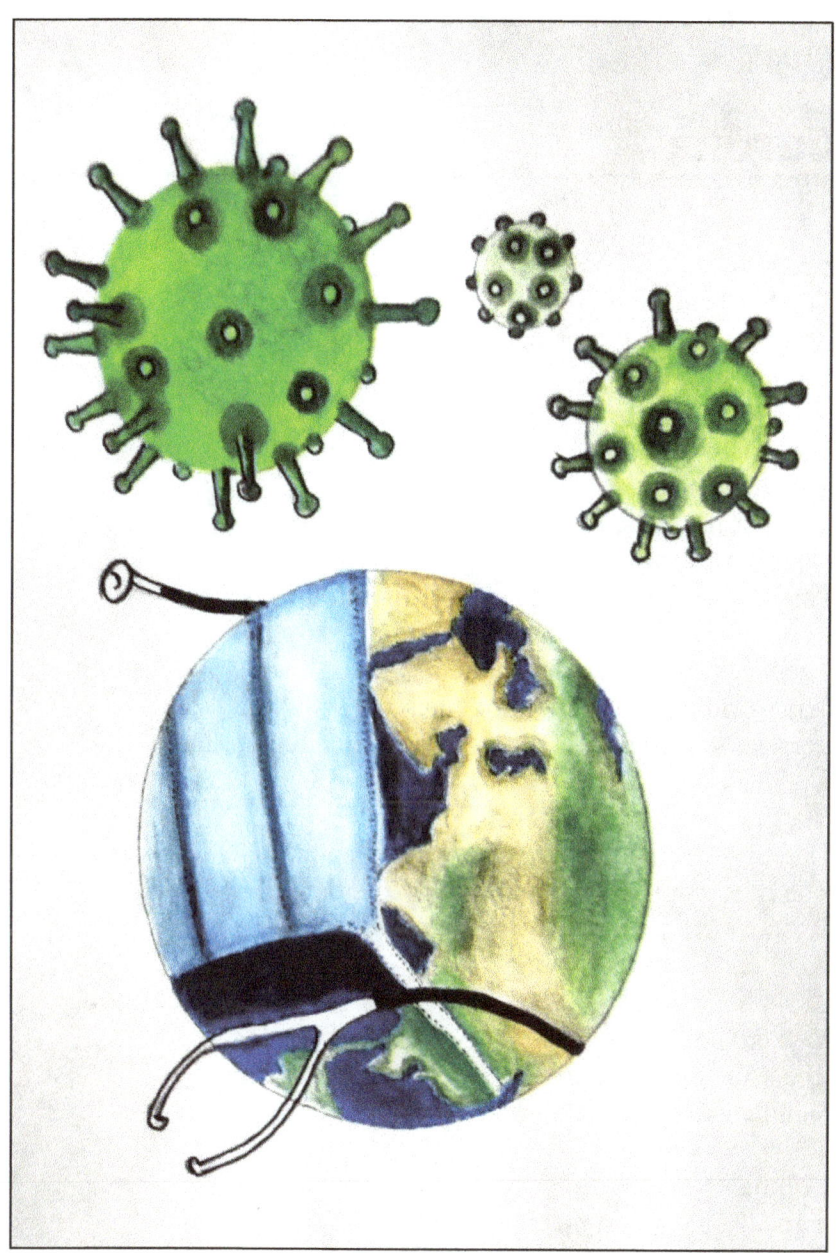

Subhadip Mukherjee *India.* **The Healing Touch**

Yogendra Munankarmy
Nepal

Corona

Today -
There is peace in the village of the town.
Zombies are being persecuted in the hopes of living.
Corona Who's Who? Cry, who? Who? S crying

Corona-
The view is six-invisible.
The war has to be fought with this.
Not with weapons;
Patience is about courage and self-control.

The world has given the halls
The world has to lose it altogether
In order to bring peace to Madhuvan on a regular basis

The current weapon against Corona
Greetings from afar with courage and patience
The rites taught by our ancestors yesterday
We now use weapons as weapons.

Corona-
You are not rich, poor king
The same behavior, all the same strikes
Which made you reckless

Corona-
You also gave us a message
To the distance of tragedy and restraint
How big, small negligence is?
A little patience and patience is how you win.

So -
Corona-you cry yourself
In wanting to control you
We do wish
We wave the setting of the flag of victory
Bye-bye Corona.

कोरोना

योगेन्द्र मुनंकर्मी

आज -

गाउँ शहर बस्तीमा मुर्दा शान्ति छाएको छ।

जीवन जिउने आशमा लाश हरुले सताईरहेको छ।

कोरोनाले सबैलाई को?को? रोना, को?को?रोना भैदिएको छ।

कोरोना-

दृश्य छ-अदृश्य छ।

युद्ध यसै संग लड्नु छ।

हतियार लिएर हैन ;

धैर्य साहस संयम र सुन्यतामा गएर भिड्नु छ।

संसार हल्लाई दिएको छ यस्ले

संसारै मिलेर हराउनु छ यसलाई

निमित्त्यान्न पारी मधुवनको शान्ति ल्याउन लाई

....

....

Yogendra Munankarmy is an international honorary member FOWPAL.USA advisor: ISSEP India. Founder advisor: Women's Hand Nepal

Daphne Muse
Oakland, CA USA

Trumpacide—

A 21st Century Pandemic
driven by nuclear narcissism,
the virus of unbridled greed,
white supremacy/nationalism,
religious zealotry,
and revulsion for things empirical.

Now deployed to destroy Black, brown,
First Nations people, immigrants,
the elderly and people with disabilities and driven by
inequities in the health care system
and Kushnarian and Milleresque tactics,
it has led to the deaths/murders of thousands of Americans
and hundreds of thousands of people around the world.

Daphne Muse is a seasoned elder, writer, poet, and cultural broker. Her work has been published in Black Scholar, The Atlantic, and aired on NPR.

Syeda Ayesha Musharraf *Pakistan*

Da Natassa Doha, Qatar

How the Pandemic Will Change Our Lives For Years to Come

In 2009, there were around 800 billionaires in the world. Within a decade, about 2019, the members of this billionaire" club" reached 2200. The great news comes for the 'Modern System,' indeed. It was said that 'money will save people.' Those who 'earned hard money,' they have the only power of protection. They have the right to live. Even in this polluted world, air purifiers, mineral water, and 'organic food' - all can be ensured by money.

But during this pandemic, it was found that the 'system' could not even protect the lives of the rich. There is a hole in the system. The world-famous art galleries suddenly closed, orchestras canceled the show; candle-light-dinner at evening has vanished, all aspects of grand elite lifestyle are under threat, such an awkward scene for an evening life.

It was thought that the slums of Asia or the villages of Africa would be desolate, but the Paris Museum or cathedrals in Spain would not be disturbed. Although China's Guangdong is attacked, Washington will be safe. Everything turned out to be wrong. By the end of this natural disaster, it is showing that the scope of 'social isolation' in the current system is just a great delusion. They did not feel it's futile to have a collective discussion of the task of strengthening the 'immune-system' of human civilization.

Elites will be able to undergo a health check-up at a costly hospital before falling into a corona attack; can isolate in the house for a long time; they do not have to worry about daily bread. Besides, there is 'e-commerce'!

164

But what will happen to the 'filthy' poor? How will the farm laborers from the shopkeepers keep going on if they stopped working? So far, the so-called 'perfect system' has failed to protect them. Irrespective of the situation, they continue to work. All rich shout in panic, 'stop everything.'

Rich has the opportunity to live well during the quarantine. That opportunity was not put in the system for the poor. It was thought that the poor could be kept away. Such social 'isolation' was demanded in the 'modern' political-economy. Farmers feed the entire economic system; their growing food provides energy to the world. Yet in this political-economy, the peasants were kept in social isolation. Workers' live' in the same situation. But in just a few weeks, people are learning hands-on: geography is interdependent, interrelated; the concept of international solidarity was once lost in the 'modern system.' This is a 'biology' that the 'economy' has overlooked. But the continued 'high growth' and global' rise in the stock market' do not guarantee any protection for the millionaires and billionaires as well. Jeff Bezos and Bill Gates, the richest men, were afraid to shake hands.

The news channels are talking about the 'global' pandemic. Still, now all global leaders are forced to admit in G20, globalization had failed terribly at different levels, who were preaching globalization one decade before irrespective of the fact they were aware that how lives of people, the national economy will be vulnerable to it. Now they are looking for humane, adaptive universal healthcare systems while selling off public healthcare to private companies, transforming the education system affordable only to rich people who will never dare to work for the poor, for the community, and for everyone. The idea of the isolation of the current capitalist system does not work anymore. In the 'age of epidemics,' there will be no health protection measures, which will guarantee the well being of the poor as well as rich. The question of good health cannot be shared among the poor and the elite anymore. It is no longer a matter of choice. It is an inevitable experience. Europe-America is learning from this experience with Asia.

The foreign virus could not be stopped at bay. How prepared are the 'society' and the 'system'? Is the medical and medicine system in the hands of several corporate institutions capable of preventing pandemics in countries avoiding the deaths of millions? Especially at the era of antibiotics, while billions of human bodies have already become drug-resistant due to excessive use of antibiotics, how the health sector will be able to handle such a situation in the future.

Natassa is an activist, writer, writing on human rights, art, and history. Occasionally writing for two publications, revolutionary democracy and people's rights

JOFRE NACHOR (Philippines)
Title: WHISPERING HOPE

This time will be remembered as the point in our history as a people when everything we have held precious and dear were challenged by this unexpected pause. The Work, the routines, the company and all the things in our own bubble of existence. Are challenged by the silent and solitary now that we are into. We are brought to reflect on the basics of our own existence, to set aside the peripherals in the likeness of wealth, power, vanity and all those we deem important and yet are in fact unnecessary for us to truly experience living.

Urmi Nipa *Bangladesh*. Watercolor painting of the effects of lockdown. The rickshaw puller, waits for passengers and dreams

Nathanael Tanko Noah
Nigeria

The Corona Salve

Records tell how much of the negative we lean.
Numbers shoot up by the day,
Humans get locked down by the numbers;
Incarcerated by our vice.
Statistics send shivers down mortal spines
Fears deliver men on moral slaughter slabs
Men who should've known better
To make well the bed, they'd be laid
Should a headache catch up to them?
The corridors of power lost their power
To minuscule forces, corruption only could escalate.
They that thought money was all,
Suddenly realized
Death comes to us all.
Regardless of social status, geography, religion, and gender.
Science could see the devastating microscopic creature
But we're as powerless against the invisible hacker
As it is futile to budge a trailer with hands.
We can't shake hands anymore
We can't hug anymore
We can't fellowship anymore.
We can't even worship together anymore
In an already strained world
We now keep social distances.
The new world order has come upon us.
I clap for you; you clap for me
I bow for you; you bow for me
Like school, children are playing games.
Even at this meeting, we sit as cowards
Worlds far apart in the same room.

Sheer will build an infirmary in 10 days.
An infirmary?
It must be the headquarters – a control center.
The Bible didn't say heaven would curse man
It merely revealed what man would do to a man.
Soon, the numbers will decline
Soon, man will triumph over virulence
Soon, man will resume his blasphemous crusade.
Soon, a great door opens to dystopia.

Ókólí Stephen Nónsó
Lagos, Nigeria

Hangmen Also Die

There's something worse than a virus
hanging around my neck
like the hangman's noose.
We're stuck in a country called a prison
Down here, children of our heroes past
are on death rolls, waiting patiently for the hangman's noose

Yesterday something lighter struck
and spread from East to West- North to South
across the length and breadth.
It knows no victim

Today, they pull their levers of hunger down,
close the doors to our mouths
and open the doors beneath our feet
to watch our bodies come to rest
like a lifeless pendulum.

They gave us air and suffocate us
with knots of hunger amidst countable ribs and hollowed sockets.
But even if they hang us all,
there's something lighter than the noose of hunger
it knows no victim
when it hits this prison- Hangmen will also die.

Ókólí Stephen Nónsó is a poet and an essayist from Nigeria. His poems have appeared in Tuck Magazine, Praxis Magazine, Adelaide Literary Magazine (New York), the best of Africa.

**Marina Novira *Beijing, China*. Novira is an Indonesian poet.
Her book** is Menyapa Rindu; *Hello, Longing.*

Deborah Nwanguma
Nigeria

Sad Music Breaking

Sad music is breaking through this half-eaten earth.
We are the center of a bruise; the world's sore is festered.
We can feel the spasms of pain, the tremor of bad news.
Lively rumors.
The dust is settling in our face, and we part our eyes in the
tumultuous rain. To see a storm.
My city-a canvas is stricken with reddish scarlet.
With a death sentence hanging above homes.
Everyone is engraved in silence, sand in throats.
we didn't see the taxi man today- anything to headache over
But the news is brewing with stories, from worry to loss.
And I can't swallow the lump that scratches at my throat.
A stubborn stain of fear.
And the smell of anxiety that chokes my dreams.
Beyond the statistics are not just numbers.
Not faceless figures
There's Doctor, the greyed one that got us, sweets- he was
martyred on Easter.
And Mother that left an early goodbye.
Beyond the statistics are nurses that fear while fighting.
Praying and hoping that their families make it as they do.
Beyond the statistics are children with lungs that fight.
In the noise, videos of a man that threw himself to the hard ground
to. A wet splattered death haunt. He had lost all-
He chewed his thumb and saw nothing to breathe for.
The aching families, lone burials, choking grief.
The end is thick with darkness with a virus.
Our hope might be the only light separating it.
Selah.

*Deborah Nwanguma is a Lawyer, a poet, and a professional
writer. She was shortlisted in the Instagram African writers'
challenge for her poem "Dead lions don't roar."*

Nuzhat Jahan Nuha Dhaka, Bangladesh. Nuha is a graphic designer. Nuha's art relates to people's emotions and fantasies. Nuha's father, a Doctor, is the inspiration for this artwork

Bolawa Sunday Ojo

COVID-19

Few days to the brink of a new year,
We got to know about a wind of pollution,
Ranging from a big corner in the East highly likely to cover the globe,
Having thought and predicted the loss, it could bring,
Nothing occurred to us as illusionary as this before!

Like the splash of a mighty ocean fighting for a wave at the sight of the storm,
Irrespective of cultural diversities, civilization, and race,
Dangerous demon that respects neither class, age nor position.
This time, it hit the whole phase with death and panic.
Isolation, quarantine, social distancing suddenly become our resort...

Nasimul Noyon Ontor Bangladesh

কোয়ারেন্টাইনে বসবাস

Living in Quarantine

একটি সোনালি দিনের কথা
মানুষগুলো সব বন্দি
আকাঁশে উড়লো পাখি
হাওয়াতে সুখের সন্ধি
বনে জাগিল কচি ঘাস
শিশির কনায় উল্লাস
মুক্ত ঘুরে কত প্রাণী
এ যে প্রকৃতির হাতছানি

বনগুলো আবার বাঁচিয়া উঠিলো
পৃথিবী দেখিল আশা
হাতি, বাঘ, ভাল্লুক, হরিণ
কত প্রাণী বাঁধিল বাসা
নদীগুলো দিল অমৃতরস

কত প্রাণী ভাসে হেসে
অথচ কদিন আগেও এরা
একোরিয়ামে ছিলো ফেঁসে

যখন মানুষের মুখে মাস্ক
প্রকৃতির বুকে স্বাস
বাতাশে নেই আর বিষ
অথচ মানুষ তুমি অদ্ভুত
এই বিষটাই করো মিস
তুমি ফিরে যেতে চাও মৃত্যুতে
অথচ ভয় পাও এই মৃত্যুর উল্লাস
ঘরে ঘরে আজ বন্দি তুমি
কোয়ারেন্টাইনে বসবাস

I'm talking about a shining day
When humans are trapped
Birds are flying in the sky
Happiness dancing in the breeze
New grass is born in the jungle
Dew rejoice in them

All animals are wandering freely
It's the blessing of nature

The jungle is reborn again
The earth now sees hope
Elephants, tigers, bears, deer
All found their home
The rivers agave nectar

All marine life is swimming and smiling
But someday ago they were trapped in an aquarium

Now humans wear a mask
Nature is free
The air is not polluted now
But humans are strange
They miss the poison

They want to go back to slow death
But fears the pandemic death
You all are now trapped in houses
Living in quarantine

Sunday Oyedeji (Easho)
Ifon, Osun, Nigeria

Though I've Heard

Though I've heard of many 'lurgies
But Covid-19 transcends medicines and technologies
Contagious more than happiness
Heartbreaking more than sadness

And the rich not becoming richer

If anyone desires to jump hereafter
Let him cuddle any COVID infected matter
Should a person desires to live longer
Let him venerate every social distancing matter

Now we'+re all infected
For every biped is seriously affected
Mothers and daughters languish in misery
Fathers and sons sprawling in poverty

Oh! God of creation
Rain panacea of mercy on every nation
We dare not smell your anger
For it's hotter than hellish fire

*Sunday is a Mass Communication final year student from Osun State
Polytechnic, Iree. A freelance journalist, teacher, writer.*

Chandrachur Pal. *Social Distancing. Artist and Assistant professor in the Electrical Engineering department*

Neerja Chandna Peters is a physician who has turned into a full-time artist and writer. This work is a collage

Jayaraj P Chennai, Tamilnadu, India

Corona

Ever since it came
Everything turned lame!
All those spreading wings,
Are now strangled strings!
A witch from East,
Plays down with peace,
While a million dreams,
Turned just dreams!
Never knew how it came
Never understood why it came
Don't know whom to blame
Everything now feels lame!
Ever since response start
We fell very long apart
Swindling in one just thought,
Don't take out the one in my heart.

Stay home. Stay safe. Leave the rest to Science

Dwilam Pal.

Giridhar Pappusetti *India* **Home: the safest place day and night while the warriors are guarding us from Covid-19.** Camlin acrylic colours. Background is painted on one sheet and the concept elements on a second sheet which was cut and pasted in respective places.

Milisha Petkar

Corona was DEFEATED

The days too eventually fell silent,
No sounds, not even by the crows,
All you could hear was the sound of
Fear knocking on the doors.

People huddled in their homes,
Bewildered and scared.
Not children, nor thieves,
To venture out, no one dared.

At night, it slipped in,
Laid its icy hands and spread the trauma,
Eventually those who left
called it Corona.

The panic grew
As the victims slowly increased.
Everyone was somehow affected,
Specially the family of deceased.

But then came that one day,
the Savior of all.
Everyone's hopes grew,
And Corona lost its gall.

The Savior had some rules.
It said to follow discipline,
Social distancing was a must,
And more important, the hygiene.

Under Savior's guidance,
the Corona vanished.

With new hope and humanity,
the Earth again flourished.
and thus,
Everyone lived,
Hoping and healthy and happy.

Rajkumar Paul. "Even Gods fear Corona."

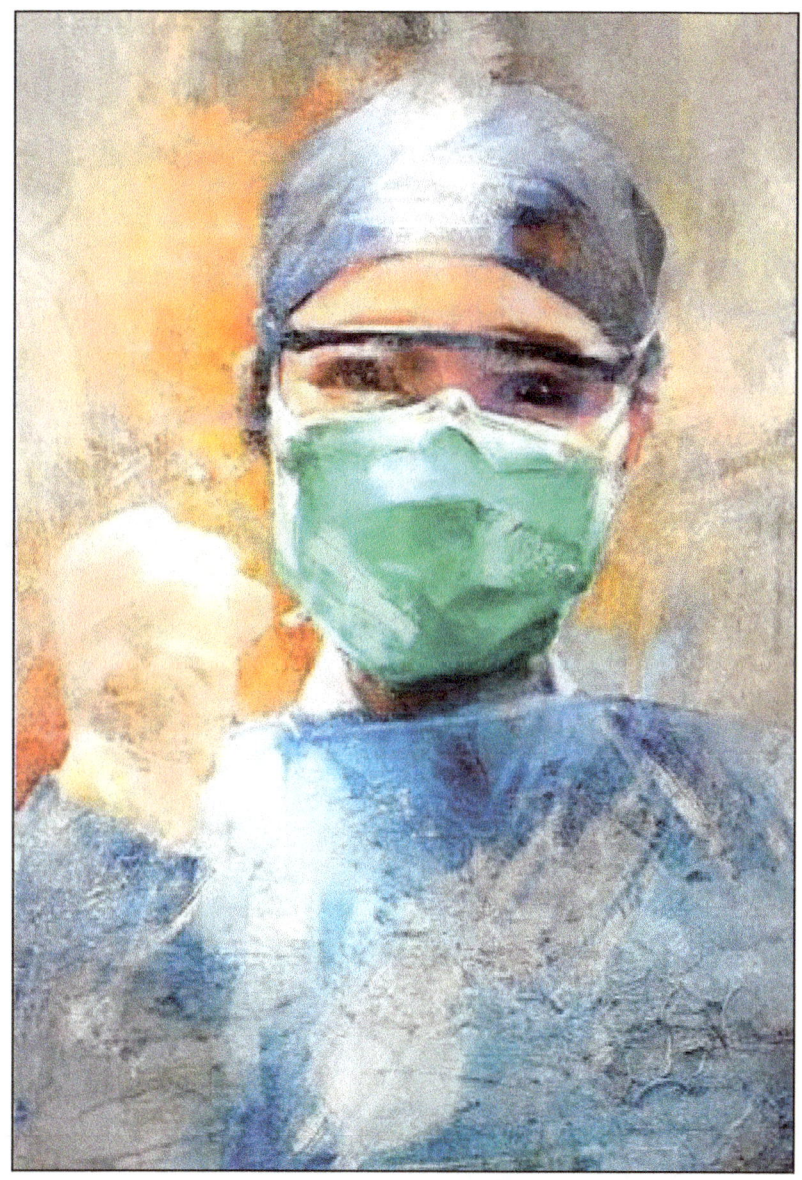

Bhawana Pokhrel *Nepal*

Geetanjali Pokhrel *India.* **Fight.** Geetanjali is a fashion student in New Delhi. A woman is wearing a mask which says FIGHT. And her head of branches are leaves which are cleaning the germs through injections and medicines. Behind it are all the humans; the rich and the poor are locked inside their houses and the virus is enjoying outside. We all are together and fighting against this virus.

Sintheva Rahman Privanka *Dhaka, Bangladesh.* **Faceless Face**

Yusup Priyasudiarja Yogyakarta, Indonesia

In Solitude

A man died in solitude
Laid with unspoken prayers from a distance
Brothers and sisters were far away
Tears rolled down their cheeks

Many others hid in fear
Many prayed for hopes
But another man died
Many more men have gone away
And no time to say goodbye

The grave is full of sadness
Homes are filled with hopeless faces
Is tomorrow another sorrow?
Another painful grief?

All are waiting for a ray of hope
from the heavenly light in their heart

Yusup Priyasudiarja has written 55 textbooks. He also writes poems and short stories. His poems are collected in the anthology "Melukis Senja" (Painting the Dusk).

Prajjol Puri **Kathmandu, Nepal**

Nightmare of Corona

यो corona को नराम्रो सपना बाट म बिउझिन आफुलाई घोच्दै छु
हाम्रा जनता पहिले भोकमारी ले मर्छन कि महामारी ले सोच्दै छु

के खान्छन ती जनता ले जो बिहान को कमाइ ले साझ खान्छन
बाहिर निस्किन हुन्न भन्छौ बाहिर सुत्नेहरु अब का जान्छन
भरी पेट तिमी सुत्दा भोकाएका ती जनता कसरी पो मान्छन
गाडी चड्ने हरु भोकाउने भए अब माग्ने ले को संग पो माग्छन

यो corona को नराम्रो सपना बाट म बिउझिन आफुलाई घोच्दै छु
हाम्रा जनता पहिले भोकमारी ले मर्छन कि महामारी ले सोच्दै छु

न कोहि भोकमरीले मरोस न कोहि महामारीले एस्तो तयारि होस्
यो समय मा कमिसन हैन हरेक नेपाली को ज्यान बक्स्योस
त्यो भोको पेट लाइ खुवाउने बारे पनि सोचियोस
अनि त्यो महामारी बाट बचाउन पनि खोजियोस

यो corona को नराम्रो सपना बाट म बिउझिन आफुलाई घोच्दै छु
हाम्रा जनता पहिले भोकमारी ले मर्छन कि महामारी ले सोच्दै छु

I am pinching myself to get up from the nightmare of corona
I am wondering if people will die from hunger or epidemic

What will they eat, who depend on daily wage to eat

Where will the people sleeping on street sleep if u r emptying the
street
How will the citizen understand if they are hungry and the
government is not
Who will people beg with, if the rich turn into a beggar

I am pinching myself to get up from the nightmare of corona
I am wondering if people will die from hunger or epidemic

Preparation should be made such that neither people die with
hunger nor from epidemic
This is not the time for commission but for saving the life
Thought should be made to feed the hungry
The plan should be made to end the epidemic

I am pinching myself to get up from the nightmare of corona
I am wondering if people will die from hunger or epidemic

Sylvia Soni Que *Germany.* **No Kisses.** @sylviasonique

Anika Tasnim Rahee, *Dhaka Bangladesh.* **Revenge of Nature 20.**
Anika is a student of Jahangirnagar University department of

Sovaizia Rahib Pakistan

Pandemic

This pandemic has made me realize
How much was left unappreciated,
The smile of a stranger,
The cry of a baby
The love of an elder
The hug of a loved one
Was all underrated
This pandemic has made me realize
What are we capable of?
Tying the old knots
Connecting with the lost cause
Praying for help
Spreading love
Being brave in the rough
This pandemic has made me realize

Writing has always been a passion of Sovaizia Rahib. She has been writing for 12 years. She used to write songs for local bands and church choir. In dark times like this, her goal is to spread a message of hope and love through my words.

Aminur Rahman/ **Dhaka, Bangladesh**

Nostalgia

I hear the jingle of chains
and lose myself in the continuous sound
of their never-ending chiming.
The intense pungency of old tobacco makes dizzy,
and once again, euphoria touches my soul.

I hear the jingle of chains
and feel invisible throughout my heart and soul.
I humble myself like many others,
craving to rise above the darkness,
but losing myself once more in deep unconsciousness.

I hear the jingle of chains.
I look for them amidst the clattering,
brace me to face them.
They hit me with greater strength,
until I feel their breath throughout my bones.

I hear the jingle of chains.
I see myself reflected in faces
that are covered by a bloody coffin,
in pebbles hidden by the earth,
and I tremble with fear,
collapsing while retreating.
Words approached me as a shackle,
fastening both my hands,
and the chain clatters, finally, gradually waning.
I hear the jingle of chains.

*Aminur Rahman has published six collections of poems in Bangla.
His work has been translated in more than twenty-five languages.*

Najma Rai Nepal

Ode to Your Smile

And the world fell silent,
nature flourished as if in a trance,
days of fresh air and starry nights turned the world lush with green,
rays of the Sun were freshly greeted like the golden Queen,
even the rivers and oceans smiled with grace,
and the world fell silent,
the silence was genuinely golden this time;

Nature felt at peace, from the oceans to the vast seven seas,
and I couldn't love it more,
joyous was our souls together,
meaning of life became more transparent,
as the world fell silent.

Shikha Raj *New Delhi, India.* Delhi based fashion designer for women's wear. Graduated from NIFT New Delhi.

Susanty Rampay *Borneo, Indonesia*

Families 2020

Once my friend asked me about
Missing our campus and our students
And I said that I didn't miss them
My friend was shocked
I asked back the meaning of missing
She ignored me

Once my mum asked me about grandma
I told to keep her at home
My mom didn't answer me
As soon as my grandma went secretly
To my uncle's house nearby
My mom was sad

Once my husband asked me about go fishing
He replied that he always be alone
All the time all the way
And I felt strangely happy
He smiled tiny

I tell you that I don't miss anyone now
I don't miss my students
I don't miss my friends
I don't miss my lipstick
I just miss my wind.

Susanty Rampay is a native of Indonesia. She teaches English at PalangkaRaya
University in the capital city of Central Borneo. She has degrees in
English Language and Literature.

Stu Reininger Calabria, Italy

A Calabrese Village Confronts the CoronaVirus

Update from the front lines of (this part of) Calabria's battle against the CoronaVirus.

The outbreak was first confined to the North, which fostered the belief that's where it would stay, considering the immediate shutdown of the affected zone.

Unfortunately, salient points were overlooked, one being that the south's most significant export has long been people, who, for the most part, emigrated north. Secondly, no matter where an Italian lives, "home" is where she was born and where her family resides. And thirdly and fourthly, telling an Italian that he or she is prohibited from going home by whatever means or at any time he or she wishes is treated as a joke or at best a minor challenge.

Consequently, the Corona Virus has reached the South and is happily propagating.

Fortunately, in our little town of 1650 souls on top of a mountain in the most remote part of the most isolated region in Italy, Corona has yet to make its appearance.

This is undoubtedly due to cooperation with strict government rules closing all gathering places, including non-necessary stores, bars, restaurants, and schools. These rules are followed rigorously by the sheep and goats, which far outnumber the people.

The residents' humans are doing their best. This includes everyone stocking up on toilet paper. Although, the bidet is ubiquitous here and hardly anyone uses toilet paper, it's understood that Americans are buying toilet paper, so it must be the right thing to do.

Also, masks and gloves are invariably worn when leaving the house. The Calabrese, however, instinctively blend modern innovation with age-old tradition; therefore, when meeting on the street, the mask and gloves are removed, hugs are given, both cheeks are kissed, mask and gloves go back on, and the conversation continues at the correct social distance.

As a further precaution, town officials are considering refilling the ancient moat surrounding the village and raising the drawbridge. Gaps in the medieval walls are being repaired, but after taking it under consideration, the council decided not to initiate defensive preparations such as archery and crossbow training.

To paraphrase President Trump, who is a source of great hilarity— and as the only American here, I am always asked to explain our particular system, which allows for the election of the occasional moron—"this virus ain't got a chance against us."

Stuart Reininger is a professional sailor. He also writes of his passions, the sea and the south of Italy. During the summer he lives and teaches maritime skills aboard his sailboat in Connecticut; he winters in a mountain village in Calabria. Stuart is originally from the Bronx in New York City.

Raiza Rhea Reponte
Hingotanan Bien Unido, Bohol Philippines

Dread of the Unknown

Like an ominous cloud traveling worldwide
this INVISIBLE spares no one
brutal to human's breath
grievously granting people's early exits.

The world tries to wrench free
from its grip
but peril looms
a glimmer of hope refuses to subside
elixir to economic woes denied.

News grows bitter each day
death tolls on the rise
eyes staring blankly at those dim rows
of our comrades swiftly ending their shows.

The days are eventually becoming silent
all you could hear are knocks
knocks of fears that haunt human's existence,
It creates doldrums leaving obscure life markings.

Hearts gloom
we're stuck in a deadly sitch
but everyone's clutching at straws
for this CROWN to dim its vibrant hues.

Raiza Rhea Reponte, 24 years old, loves writing. She writes to understand the language of the soul; loosen the ties of melancholia.

Urba Riazi, *Bangladesh* **Fire and Ice.**

Rashley Rioveros *Philippines*. **Pandemic**

I am **Syeda Afrukhtah Rippy**, art and design (A level teacher). Bangladesh

Heather Romero-Kornblum
USA

Shopping For an Apocalypse:

the logic of 'Doomsday Preppers' on TV
mostly middle-class or rich white men
    afraid of an electromagnetic
shift
in the earth's poles
or communism
instruct their wives
on freeze-drying
    deer meat as they worry about being hunted
this new virus
does not distinguish
between the haves and have nots
does not care about your color
    does not care
if the apocalypse is only in your head
San Francisco
I wait online at Whole Foods
with a couple of mangos
    pineapples
    a tri-tip
the yogurt has been cleaned out
'What do you buy for an apocalypse?'
    I joke with the cashier
thank my past self
for having the tendency to load up on cans when they're on sale
I have enough Annie's to outlast this
at 1 am
I cook the tri-tip
    mix lentils and quinoa
I wonder if this was what Pompeii was like

They'll find me
    frozen
    in the kitchen
    spatula in hand
    husband and son asleep
    fridge full

Heather Romero-Kornblum is a San Francisco researcher and writer. Heather has been a featured poet at The WordParty Poetry and monthly Jazz series, Sacred Grounds – the longest-running open mic in San Francisco, and Mutiny Radio.

Michael Rothenberg
USA

Corona Confessions

(excerpts)

It's not my business how everyone dies.
One coyote barks, howls, yip yip, sounds
like a pack screeching wild on the lakeshore.

"The caissons go rolling along..."
We are buried where we fall.
We march across the hilltop at dusk.
A pyre of strawberry ash at the mall.

This morning my dark night of the soul.
Go to sleep, nasty angels! The Terribles are troubling.
They will deliver us unto an incurable ambivalence.

Still, I'm waiting for aliens from outer space to come to
save us from the pandemic. They will come in starships
loaded with toilet paper, firing cosmic hand sanitizer cannons.
Tonight look up to the skies, and you will see them coming.

How can you sleep when you know there's a crisis?
It's a survival instinct to stay alert, be on guard,
to figure out solutions, be ready, to protect and defend,
when the shit hits the fan.

Meanwhile, I am going to take a breather from the Civil War.
I'm gonna go have a piece of chocolate cake.
Wash my hands. Eat a bag of potato chips.
Wash my hands. Head down to the lake with the dog.
Wash my hands. Draw a meaningless picture.
Wash my hands. I am not learning anything new here.

208

Wash my hands. It gets sadder and sadder by the minute.
Wash my hands. The bloodshed is horrifying.
Wash my hands. I have had enough of the punditry and rage.
I am going to go wash my hands.

Rothenberg is a poet and artist, and co-founder of 100 Thousand Poets for Change. His most recent books of poetry include Drawing The Shade (Dos Madres Press, 2016), Wake Up and Dream (MadHat Press, 2017), and a bi-lingual edition of Indefinite Detention: A Dog Story (Varasek Ediciones Madrid, Spain, 2017). He lives in Tallahassee, Florida, where he is Florida State University Libraries Poet in Residence

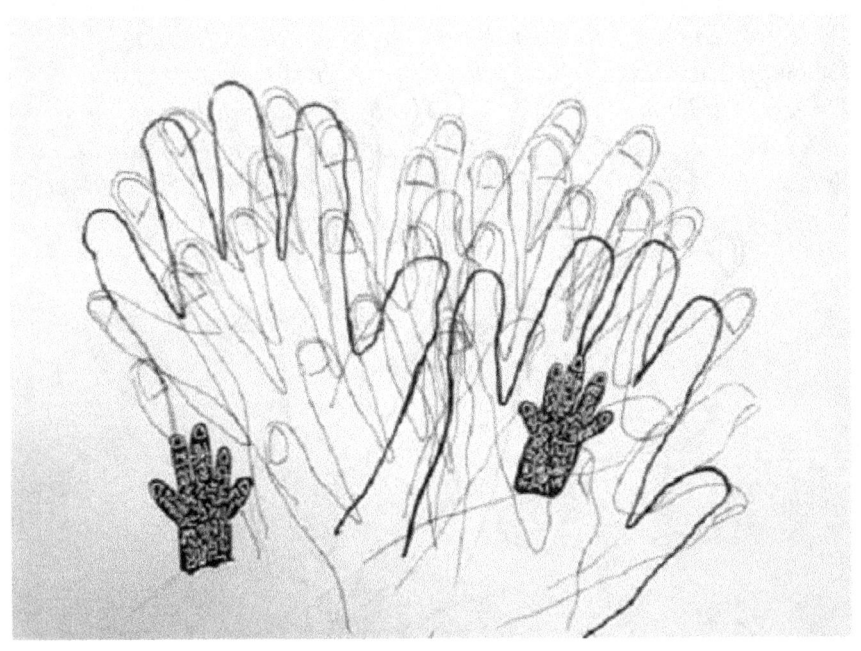

Michael Rothenberg," Wash Your Hands"

Sweta Routray India "The grieve"

Sweta Routray India

Covid-19

A tear rolled down her cheek
It touched the Earth and created the river of tears.
Her waiting eyes met her son after so many years,
Tears rolled down her cheeks as they realized the good relationship
we share with our loved eyes.

Her waiting eyes met her ten years' daughter in that isolated world,
Tears rolled down her cheeks as she cannot touch her loved ones.
Her waiting eyes have not got a job for the last four days,
Tears rolled down her cheeks as she cannot feed her loved ones.
Her waiting eyes saw her kid in video conferencing,
Tears rolled down her cheeks as she has dedicated her 24*7 for the
nation and cannot spend time with her loved ones.

Her tired, waiting eyes are now numb and relaxed as global
footprint has decreased a bit,
Tears rolled down her cheeks after seeing the Death Valley as she
cannot save loved ones.
And here among all these, we are living with "Question marks,"
why? How? And What next?

Sweta Routray a Student at B. architecture at NIT, Rourkela

Madhuparna Roy Kolkata, India

Unlock Your Treasures

Unlock your treasures,
Oh, Guardians of Wealth;
Now is the time to donate!
For we've donated to you
in surplus for centuries
And it's been lying with you,
Secured under lock-'n'-keys!

Silvers and golds
and diamonds and cash,
are overflowing your vaults
We know
Unlock your treasures,
Oh, Guardians of Wealth;
In front of whom you bow!

It pains me
to see men suffering
from diseases unknown.
It hurts more to know.
that charity once has given
hardly comes back,
To help the 'believers', though!

Unlock your treasures,
Oh, Guardians of Wealth;
Just donate
as much as you wish
'Coz God neither wants
treasures for Himself;
Nor likes a golden niche!

Plague 2020

Unlock your treasures,
Oh, Guardians of Wealth;
It's time to set
Those treasures trove free
'Coz nothing's more trivial
Then holding onto it,
and deserting Adam's tree!

Unlock your treasures,
Oh, Guardians of Wealth;
Give those gems back
to the wretched society . . . .
Open the flood gates
of the 'House of God',
Return 'charity' to Humanity!

Unlock your treasures,
Oh, Guardians of Wealth;
You once taught us to give.
We're dying of virus' unknown
So now, I would like to receive it!
The dear Vatican, Kaaba n Tirupati -
I'm sure you still believe in charity.

Madhuparna Roy is a teacher by profession. She is passionate about penning down her thoughts regularly. She expresses herself both in English and Bangla, her mother tongue.

In this poem, she earnestly wishes the human race to survive a possible extinction against the dreaded attack of the unknown virus. She hopes the "Houses of God" all around the globe, in front of whom man bows his head and joins hands together to give up ALL they have gathered so far through charity.

Beenish Saeed Lahore, Pakistan

Today I Breathe, Today I Am Different

The Pakistani air was never this distressed, the joy, the laughter, where was it all? How naive were we to think that this merciless and malicious world would move on, brutality had taken root in the muds of this country, no child was safe, especially Asad, a nine-year-old boy who had nothing to cover up and with no one to beg to, he was stranded, starving and slowly melting away in compromises. Compromises? They were a two-way street for Asad each day; he would not eat food, walk barefooted on the streets, frostbiting his skin, almost as if it was torturing him for being alive in this menacing time. God, He was the only one that the young soul could look up to, but to his dismay, no reply came. Lying famished and fatigued was nothing new for him, and this day was no different. He lay on the streets of Old Lahore, eyes fluttering closed as his strength slowly gave way; until he heard a deep voice calling him "Boy, get up, how do you expect to lie here without a mask or sanitizer, now run along to your Baba!" How could Asad tell him that he had no one but a pitiless Uncle who would beat him up when he came home without money, he tried cleaning cars' windows and even sell the handmade drawings that his sister Ayesha had taught him, but she too had died, she was raped and thrown in a garbage bag, reminding her that a girl belonged there in a society like this. "Sir, I have no one, I am too poor to afford anything, please help me, I beg you, and may God give you seven sons, for the sake of Allah, please give me something to eat!" He cried, tears flowed down his cheeks like a river that had newly broken inside him, hope slowly floated away and death, oh how Asad wanted to die, to get away from all this. "Come with me, boy; I'll help you if you work in my factory. I'll pay you 250 rupees per each hour. Sound like enough, boy?" A malicious grin spread on the man's face, but

Asad's innocence, like a newly blossomed flower-covered each flaw that everyone else had. After walking for a few miles, the man showed him a dingy factory that was old, and no one was inside it. "Go inside, work is waiting for you, and boy, don't you dare tell anyone about the work I am going to give to you!" the man hissed. He grabbed Asad by the arm and pushed him inside, "Sir, there is no one ever here, what work do I have here," Asad's voice coming in sobs, he was not the kind of person who would be scared, but fear had slowly penetrated inside his veins. The -210- man grabbed a whiplash, and whatever came next had nothing but scars to give, emotions to build and innocence to take. Asad lay on the cold factory floor, his limbs hurting, legs giving away and eyes filled with tears. His breath came slowly, and his head spun to the melody of disgrace, who could he talk to, revealing this pain that had much more to it than what meets the eye. "Asad love, look here, Mummy is here to pick you up, I am sorry that I left you here in the first place, come, my son, there is a better place in this world for you, there always was!" An angelic voice echoed in his ears that raised goosebumps. "Mama is that you, mama, why did you leave me here in this hell, you must hate me for what happened, Mama, I am sorry I couldn't stop him, I tried!" His mother wiped his tears away and smiled at him before carrying Asad towards a white light, she grinned at him, a longing complete. This COVID 19 pandemic has hit us all in different ways, but minimum wage workers have been affected immensely, in these strenuous times, it is our responsibility to be intrepid and raise our voices on platforms like the social media because this pandemic is not an excuse for sexual abuse and rape in any way, shape or form. First-year of O-Levels at Lahore Grammar School Senior Girls Campus OPF. She is fourteen years old and says she wants to present a true picture of Pakistani people all across the globe.

Lena Rushing San Luis Obispo, CA. 5/5/20. Contemporary-narrative artist and curator. Rushing's work typically features a strong, unconventional female presence and relies heavily on

Ananya Guru Sangameshwar
South India

Face Yourself!

And we are all forced
To stay home, stay isolated,
Why are we afraid?

For, we had sought
Escape in all those worldly pursuits,
And social connections.
They gave us meaning,
They gave us direction,
And now we are left
With only ourselves.

And we are afraid,
To confront the person
We have to live with our whole life,
We don't want to be left alone
With our dark thoughts.

Hidden Hopes,
Latent fears,
Unfulfilled promises,
Untapped talent.

It's time,
To look at yourself in the eye,
Face all that you've been hiding within,
Face it!

And once you face it,
Embrace it.
For it's time to discover yourself,
It's time to recreate yourself
And learn to accept it

218

And love it too.

So what if it's social distancing,
Get closer to yourself!

For today is a new day,
Who knows what tomorrow will bring?

Sangameshwar is a budding teen writer and her first poetry book
"Unfettered: A
Collection of Poems" was published in 2019. She is passionate about
music and
enjoys singing.

Sanchita Roychowdhury India. Man Vs Virus

Abubakr Terkimbi Saidu/ Nigeria

Thomases

With the sending of millions

To their grave, early grave!

And counting and still counting
And causing the lockdown of the world.
Crippling the economy of the world
And sending the world
The whole wide world
To its knees.
And everything, absolutely everything
Coming to a standstill,
Many here tagged COVID-19 a scam here!
THOMASES, DOUBTING THOMASES
With this in mind
They go their way, normal way:
Of crowding
Of hugging
Of kissing
Of hand shaking
And sneezing, unprotected sneezing
With a word accompanying:
COVID-19 is a scam!

THOMASES, DOUBTING THOMASES

If…
Even if… you're there
You're there for the class
And not, certainly not for the class-less!

Mohan Singh Saud/ Nepal

COVID-19

COVID-19
Mohan Singh Saud

Coronavirus first appeared in Wuhan China
Spreading the world like a flame of fire
WHO calling it pandemic
Named COVID-19.

It should have been as it is
Humans exploiting the nature
In the name of development
Building massive constructions.

Over migration leaving hometown
In the name of globalization
Forgetting own culture
In the name of modernization.

People living with biodiversity
Meshing with nature
Having cultural diversity
And linguistic diversity are humans.

Forgetting all these
And living with luxury
In the skyscrapers in cities
Eating poisonous foods.

Polluting the environment
Getting cosmetic beauty
Enjoying with artificial nature
Living with junk foods.

Rich countries investing in nuclear bombs
Inviting cold war competing with others
Running after money following capitalism
Forgetting humanity and socialism.

Human encroachment on nature
Destroying the habitat of creature
Seeing the foolishness of humans
Perhaps the Almighty created corona.

Humans are the sole cause of COVID-19
It has come to teach many things to them
Saying 'back to nature' and more
Cultivating humanity in humans!

Saila Sarmin-Rapti Dhaka, Bangladesh. Miss ME! After completing a degree in Economics, Saila is working to balance her real world and her creative, imaginary world

SWADHINA SARANGI, India

Vandana Sawani

The Poet Quarantined, I am

O blessed Bird!
I am quarantined, and you are free
The whole world you can see
Free-spirited you fly
Over the garden and atop the banyan tree
O blessed Bird!
Quarantined I am
Stifled in the space of my home
Lonely and alone
With nowhere to roam
O blessed Bird!
You flap your wings
And fly across the vastness of the sky
Inside the four walls of the house
I end up with a painful cry
O blessed Bird!
My wings are not broken
Yet I cannot fly
I ruffle the feathers to take the flight
Alas! you know my sad plight
O blessed Bird!
I sing a lonely song
In the house, I am caught
I have done no wrong
Yet I feel lonely and distraught
O blessed Bird!
I am quarantined, and you are free
The whole world you can see
Free-spirited you fly

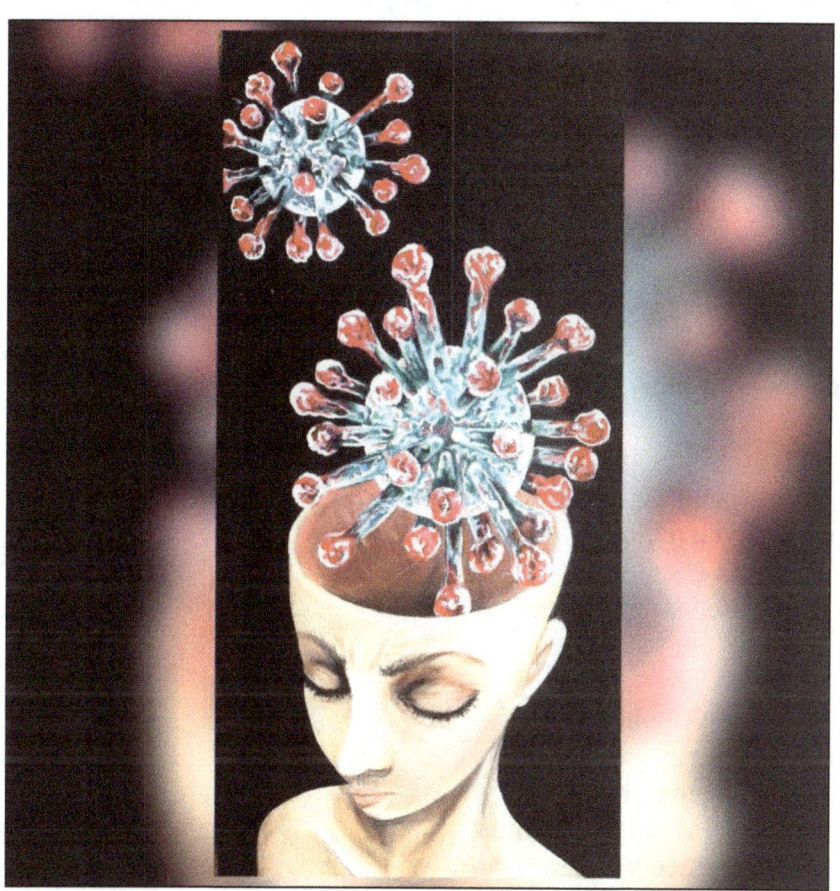

Minnette Schmidt South Africa

Chris Scully Devon, UK

Covid-19

It's not the cough that will carry you off
It's the coffin they'll carry you off in
Or at least that's how it used to go but now
I'm not so certain

There's panic in the supermarkets
Fear on every aisle
No hope for loo roll bread or milk
In any shop for miles

The pubs are shut
The gym is gone
What are we all to do
The old are trapped
The young are lost
The hospitals are screwed

The worlds have gone mad
But it's not all bad
Just take a breath to relax
Just stay at home and if you must
Walk old forgotten tracks

This is just nature's way of sorting things
It seems we stepped too far
She's just making sure we stay in check
The world needs time to reset
Stay Home
Stay in
Stay calm

The world will heal as we shall to
Together we will survive
And once this is all done and through
We and nature will thrive

Scully is a bus stop bard, commuter, & muser, new to the world of poetry and still finding his feet. Taking inspiration from fellow commuters and the views from bus windows.

Yassin Senge
Tanzania, United Republic

The Darkest Cloud

Still, I can imagine
However, I am blind!
When I hear of COVID nineteen
As the darkest cloud
Suffocating the whole world in the quarantine
And freezing millions of people's blood
I can listen to painful screams of children
Crying for groaning mothers in the cloud
Everything is shut down
How shall we eat
Without sweat?
We as men
Everyone is locked down
Who to prove beyond a reasonable doubt?
Whether we are guilty or innocent
All in the quarantine prison
Ooh my God, why?
Doctors die
No cure which is sure
Children cry
Soldiers die
It's a third world war

Shafiya Shafi , Kashmir. I am Shafiya, from Kashmir.
I work as a freelance artist mostly doing abstracts,
conceptual art and illustration.

**Khairah Shah *Trinidad and Tobago* Social Distancing. Khairah is
15 years old.**

Tanisha Kaushal **India**

Stay at Home

The white mask chokes the policeman.
It drags to the memory,
Of the long and conical mask
Concealing the doctor's face
Among the Black Plague's days.
15 dead? Oh, look!
A few hundred may lay dead,
A few thousand gasping for breath.

The coffin of the children's favorite old man,
Lay among thousands.
Once in long years,
Rome's streets appear alone.
More than death devastates empty shelves.
With no work, lay the city's poor
Already acclaiming themselves, dead.
Yet, the bird's chirps seem louder,
Each breath feels lighter
And the sky seems brighter. The healers stare,
Their faces scarred, red with sweat
 Each work, to heal, clinging to hope
Even when there seems To be no cure.
Yet the city's waste is dumped,
The sewage water does not flood,
And food settles in stomachs.
And each pray to no god, but one another.
 How to win this war?
You ask, child? stay at home!
Oh, yes! Stay at home.

Sheena Shamoon Islamabad, Pakistan

I wanted to be Batman!

When I was a kid, I used to watch all these superheroes saving the world from evil, and I just wanted to be like them, but all of them had some super-human powers that I did not. My mother told me that her favorite superhero was Batman, care to know why? Because he did not have any superpower but still was a superhero. She told me that you need no superpowers to be a superhero; you just have to dream about it.

There's a saying, '*You like because you love despite*' and it doesn't just apply to people. It goes for everything. When I decided to opt for medicine as my career, I liked it because this profession was charming, graceful, and respected. When the coronavirus pandemic started, this was the time I realized I loved my profession as much as I liked it, this was my time to become batman, a superhero without any superpowers.

If Wearing a protective gear that doesn't allow your body to breath, a mask that doesn't allow you to speak, goggles that hide the sparkle in your eyes and gloves that make your fingers ache, standing without a break for 8 hours and treating people who were now not just some patients I had taken an oath to help but family, doesn't make you a superhero, what will! If going to the hospital every day with the same enthusiasm without a pinch of regret or confusion, without a pint of frustration or anger but with a soul full of hope and a heart full of empathy doesn't make you a superhero, what will! If spending all of your time taking care of other people's families and not knowing how your own family was, doesn't make you a superhero, what will!

234

When we are kids, we don't know what profession is good and what is bad, but we just want to be like someone we adore. Imagine now how inspiring would this be for some 10-year-old girl to see a woman become bat-woman in front of her very eyes, how truly awakening would it be for a little boy who wishes to become a superhero, that you need no superpowers but just a dream and some passion for making a difference in the world. My work as a bat-woman is a million times harder than when I was just a doctor, but it's also a million times better because I get to become the superhero I always wished to be. You know what they say about being a doctor. *If it were easy, everyone would do it because it's the best job in the world, despite everything, because of everything.*

Sheena Shamoon is a student of 4th-year MBBS, writer and painter.

Rashmi Sharma *Guwahati, India.*

As I Draw My Eyes

As I draw my eyes open, I see green
Dewdrops and blossoms delicate,
Meadows with blue butterflies fluttering round and round
The smell of first rain and the red sunset
The ground laden with strawberries, the first grain harvest
When is the last time I have smelt strawberries?
I don't remember the last time I have dived in its smell,
I knew that the sweetness was too hard to forget as I tasted it.
When is the last time I have dipped my feet
In rock blue pool of water that come crashing through hills
As I bent down to touch the sunset on the water
A moment of my own and just my own.

But the earth seems to be upset now,
Tired, ailing, and debilitated.
A little mad, a little pity for us.
And all of a sudden the dream break into pieces
As I close and open my eyes again
To find me with four walls staring blank at me
The creeks of floors seem to haunt my existence.
Routing after the little efforts to heal others and self.
The glaring screen and few books
Straining my eyes to pain every blinks
But little did it rest while running across fields and mountains.
The silence is unbearable but hopeful.
Hoping that another sunrise will bring news
Of freedom and love, little more empathy, and little less pain.

Sheena Shamoon

i am called Thupten, a full time Artist, originally from
Tibet, currently a refugee. Art is not for entertainment,

Thupten Shasimo, The Time Uninvited

and certainly not about beauty, it is about questioning
the statusquo and in search of the truth.

238

Ehsan Shayegh Iran/ Italy

βeta Human

I had to do something to finalize my exhibition; it could be a script settling down on the platform of desert laying on the ground of the gallery. I was immersed in my thoughts and putting them on words when all of a sudden, there was a knock on the door. As I replied, the voice said it was Corona. Since I had no idea who it was, I did not open the door. A day after, I happened to know that there was a similar knock on the door of everyone else in the city.

Some opened the door, but some not.

I was gradually getting familiar with Verona city and making friends. We were shaking hands and hugging each other warmly. Currently, we have to express our feelings simply by sending some stickers and looking at the passing spring from the window of our digital displays in front.

In Ceramic Science, when we put the mug inside the drying oven and pass it through a temperature of eight-hundred, we believe that there is a shift in its phase, i.e., there is a shift from α phase to β phase. In other words, after cooking, it is not called mud anymore. Furthermore, it does not carry the characteristics of the mud either. Regardless of what form it used to have before leaving the oven, it does not hold the very characteristics of the mud, and it is contracted stuff with novel characteristics.

I think the recent events have created the same shift in our phase, from α human to β human. Sooner or later, there would be no trace of the CoronaVirus. Are we going to think about the destructive effects of climate change, whose effect and speed is more than CoronaVirus, during this quarantine period, with this much access to information and news from past to present? And is this β human, the frightened one, who is worried about his death and surviving methods, going to do something in order to preserve the environment in the Post-Corona period? Or like that α human, he is going to look at forest fires and animals burning behind the digital displays. Finally, he will utter: "WHAT A PITY…"

Ehsan Shayegh, Social Distancing

Osatogbe Shola
Nigeria -West Africa, Africa.

Covid - 19

On your mark, ready, let's go!
Accusations and counter-accusations
Those that are supposed to find a cure are acting officious pointing
accusing fingers
The body count on the increase and the fear is gripping
Hearts bleeding
I hope you all can hear me loud and clear
I have to clear the air cause it's filled with a lot of stenches
And the truth is my wrench
I am talking like a talking drum and beating it hard enough until it
is like I am virtually banging on your eardrum.

Some are pants sagging
Others are hands clapping
Eyes teary cause things are becoming scary
The rulers are shagging their subjects and electorates
Everybody is at a loss
In a lose-lose situation
There is no victor or vanquish
The fear we must banish and responsiveness we all must embrace
This plague must be faced headlong before it can be phased out.

Man-made or as a natural consequence of cross-transmission
A product of deceit or conceived out of deceit
This is the Coronavirus
Heads are spinning in a gyroscope.
The butcher showing no discrimination
It's all out for total annihilation
This is not like your everyday Sci-fi or a well-scripted horror
movie

The horrors are real
The harrowing effects are more real than life
This is like none other and its different from the others: The
Plague, Zika, Ebola, HIV/AIDs and the SARs virus respectively
In all respect it is vicious
Everywhere is in lockdown
Perhaps this is the final countdown to Apocalypse.

Osatogbe Shola,is 39 years old,has a Bachelor's degree in Science Education from the University of Ilorin, and is a professional teacher.

Paul Siekor
Cornwall, United Kingdom

Self-Isolation

Look at me
I'm just fine
Says the washing
Doing the can-can on the line

Look at me
I don't even blink
When you pour hot water on me
Says the kitchen sink

Look at me
I'm all right Jack
Says my keyboard
When I bash the keys on my Mac

Look at us
We'll stick around
Say the dandelions
Yellow teeth poking above ground

Look at me
I'm always replete
Says the dustbin
Three bags full complete

Look at me
I don't recognize you
Says the mirror
Reflecting only what is true

Paul Siekor is the pen name of an autistic writer who was diagnosed with Asperger's at the age of 61. He is working on a book about autistic identity, a memoir and a volume of poems.

Asmaul Husna Simi
Dhaka, Bangladesh

Suffocation in Quarantine

Suffocation in Quarantine I

In a beautiful evening – when Elvis Presley's *Can't help falling in love* plays in the background – I am enjoying every bit of the moment and beat of the music and also feeling suffocation inside four walls, what would I do? I take refuge in the sea of emotions. Closing my eyes, I open the door of my mind and slowly step towards the sea. The wind starts to play with my hair, the waves with my touch, and the sunset with my mind. The sea breathes heavily and gives long sighs, burdensome ones. Thousands of years' existence has made her heavy, and she weeps with her sorrow. Her heart beats with every wave, like the rhythm of the train.

The setting sun is in a hurry to be lost here and found somewhere else. Seagulls are paving their way to somewhere unknown. None is caring about anything. The sea doesn't care about the sun, the sun doesn't care about seagulls, the seagull doesn't care about time, and time doesn't care about me. In this world of nothingness, the darkness crawls. It comes with baggage, a heavy one.

The more moments pass, the more darkness deepens, however, can't rule long as 'the star' peeps. Another hundred stars follow thousands, and then millions. Gently, they drink heaviness from the water, and the sea feels lighter, like the feathers. It flows and whispers to the wind, "Can't help falling in love."

Suffocation in quarantine II

While we're encaged in four walls, our dear cities breathe fresh, the dolphins play joyfully in the sea, and the birds fly at their hearts.

Human beings' sabbatical time has opened the world for those who remain deprived of their natural share. The million-year-old world seems young with her nature.

Such a time when humanity is at war with tiny particles, the sun sets for many without any sunshine. Hopeless and helpless are potent words in the dark days. Our own hands are the bearer of our enemies. The messenger of emotions – warmth, touch, hug, and kiss – becomes the source of death for some or many.

A time when a part of human beings exhibit utmost humanity, a part encapsulated in fear, a part engraved in panic, and a part caged in selfishness. Each is trying their best to laugh, love, and live. None is aware of how many of us can fight till the last. The fight may last long; however, we're adapting to make it short. The majority of us will survive. We will live the rest of our lives with memories, haunted and loved ones, of these closed-door days.

In a time when technology is connecting us, entertaining with viral videos, songs, and dances, energizing with messages, inspiring with stories, and shaking with the news. Even after all these, our boredom prevails, frustration rules, and depression deepens.

In the back of our minds, we prepare ourselves for good days ahead. We dream of the days to reunite with loved ones, travel the beautiful destinations, visit eateries and coffee shops, and feel human emotions. We impatiently wait for a beautiful spring of our life.

Suffocation in quarantine III

A generation is leaving us, a generation is becoming too heavy to hold the burdens, and a generation is struggling to survive. One generation passes wisdom, love, and humanity to another. The chain has become brittle these days. How much kindness can hold the world together, none can predict.

The coffins, fresh flowers, and deadly silence are hovering around our minds. Mostly, our days are serving and sustaining for unpleasant realities. Death has become a layer of the white canvas where we don't dare to paint, and life has become a layer of black cover where we keep ourselves hidden, untouched, and unwelcoming.

An evening is there to bear the twilight. The birds are chirping while returning to their nest, empty roads are slowly awakening by the yellow lights, and the dogs are barking somewhere perhaps to remind them they're accompanying us. The trees, buildings, and cities are static while the leaves and time are mildly moving.

These dark moments have led ways for us to be with families, friends, lovers, and ourselves or wherever and with whomever we reside. The beauty of life and death are together. Can we hold this togetherness? Can we uphold our economy? Can we treasure this humanity? Can we value this love? Can we fight the battle with this tiny particle?

Working as a Publication Associate at the Centre for Policy Dialogue (CPD), based in Dhaka, Bangladesh. I write poems, short stories, features and newspaper articles. I perform my poetry in open mic shows in Dhaka. Crafting words, seeping coffee and trotting around the globe are my forte for living life.

Ritika Mittal / Mumbai
Mumbai India

Remember

Remember, last spring?
When you were on the swing
Pivoting it higher and higher
To see the clouds come nearer.

Remember, last spring?
When your friends were
just a call away
Traffic is the only delay.

Remember, last spring?
When you would complain
the sun is too hot
And wanted to stay inside.

Remember, yesterday?
When you looked out of your window
At the flying birds
And felt the need for freedom.

Remember, yesterday?
When instead of cinema
With buddy it was
Movie night with the family.

Remember, yesterday?
When even the air conditioner
Didn't give the satisfaction
You knew the sun would give.

Do you remember?
You should because when you go out
And you will after you pay for your sins
You will know what you crave.

Ritika Mittal is an eighteen-year-old woman from India pursuing a career in
commerce with writing and reading as hobbies.

Elizabeth Ralph-Smith *Originally from New Zealand, Elizabeth
is a traditional artist currently studying at The Florence Academy of
Art, Italy. This piece was painted during the Covid-19 lockdown period*
to show the beauty which still exists in simple spaces.

Peddina Sripriya
Bengaluru, India

Together We Can

When we used to think about Heroes,
We were reminded of those
Wearing armors of gold
Carrying weapons of steel
Seeing the sea of bloodshed
Killing without any second thought
To protect their people and their country from enemies
But now our Heroes and She-roes also wear an armor,
Their shield is PPE
They are the front line workers
Fighting the global Pandemic and saving lives
Selflessly serving others without any second thought
But what can we do to help them?
Let's follow the rules of lockdown;
Stay home, stay safe without any frown,
Maintain social distancing and wear a mask;
Well, it's not such a big task,
Compared to those in front line working tirelessly;
We are doing good, let's continue religiously,
This situation has proved that we are all one;
Even if we belong to different religions, we are all humans,
We need to help others in whatever way we can;
Avoid disposables cause protecting Mother Earth is our plan,
Let's hope and pray,
This, too, shall pass and show us a new day!

Peddina is a final year BBA Finance and Accountancy student in Christ (Deemed to be University), Bengaluru, India. She is a Fellow from the Insurance Institute of India (FIII)

Tanvi Gaurav Srivastava/ Gujarat

Quarantine Chime...!

The main door
of the old world has shut
and all new shoes came back
to the rack after the rush.
Lives-vibes get shut down
measurable amounts of dust have been
destroyed from books
they shine now, strutted with its crown.

Only a tiny skylight has many possibilities.
from where a cuckoo can
peep and sing.
From where a few drops of rain can
drench our need to drink.
From where a ray of sunshine can
unfold the hopes outright.
From where a dusky fallen star can
stick and twinkled fortnight.

Tanvi Gaurav Srivastava, a teacher, is best known for her poems & sketches. Her poems have been published in various national & international anthologies. She has her den in Vadodara, Gujarat, India.

They shudder at a touch,
An embrace, a kiss,
Even of shadows.
All of them.
I now know why
Venus is moving far,
Far away from the moon
Every second,
Inch by inch.

Harshita Srivastava India. Corona Diaries. Harshita is a student at
St Xaviers University in Kolkata

Virgil Suárez *USA* **Wash Your Hands**

Virgil Suárez Florida, USA

Wash Your Hands

gather the poems
you've always wanted
to read

reread as if
your life depended
on words

to lift you
beyond the here
now

shower often
sing, meditate
see how your

hands turn
to swans
about to embrace

Suárez is a Professor, MFA, Louisiana State University (1987), specializing in creative writing and Latino/a (especially Cuban-American) literature. Poet, essayist, novelist, and short story writer, Professor Suarez is the author or co-author of over fifteen books of poetry and prose. His latest book is *90 Miles (Selected & New Poems)*, University of Pittsburgh Press, 2005. His work was featured in the *W.W. Norton Anthology of Latino/a Literature*, 2010.

VS Sudiptha India. 6th grade. Due to the lockdown , kids are engaged with drawing & paintings. This MahMag submission allowed us to learn about how to be safe during Covid-19 and drawing.

Kimi Sugioka
San Francisco, USA

Princess

The princess cruise ship
docked in the bay
lights up at night
reminding us that
COVID-19 or sars-2
is not leaving
anytime soon

it is strangely
comforting
to write my will
with signatory
witnesses

My teaching assistant
of 18 years
is fuming mad
because I suggested
that she uses a chrome
book from the classroom

She is livid because
she thinks that I
I am asking her to
go to school

Suggestions
are not recommendations
Can anyone tell the
difference anymore?

The sky is storm grey
a cold wind
blows from the princess
shifting waters while
seagulls martial the shore
as if to say
This is ours now.

Kimi Sugioka, educator, songwriter, poet, mother, and lover of cats, rabbits, and birds, has published two books of poetry, the newest of which is "Wile & Wing" on Manic D Press.

M. Anton Sulistyo
Jakarta, Indonesia

Memento Vivere

before winter ends in Queens
even in dreams I never suspected
visited by a plague named feminine, Corona
but not like the prophecy in the book of revelation
no horned creature winced
with a curiously face, muttered:
"When can I come to pick up your soul?"

there are no angels flapping their wings
as if to give a warm hug, whispering softly:
"memento vivere!"
before winter ends in Queens
I entered the odd room in my head
where there are many rows of entrances
but there is no door to the outside
from alienation
and mute atmosphere

like a cocoon before incarnating
as a butterfly, confused, I wonder:
"Is this the beginning of a journey to the noetic realm
or the last outing before moksha?"
The question brushed off reason
to the dark corner of the mind. Makes me tired
and desperate looking for keywords other than faith
Corona is still resting
in my silent world of sleep.

Notes: Memento Vivere is a Latin phrase = remember to live.
Moksha is a Hindu phrase = the transcendent state attained as a
result of being released from the cycle of rebirth.

Christian Paul S. Sunga
Philippines

Good Riddance

We're birds in a quest going through a labyrinth and path
Caged, exposed, and with response unable to find out
In a shadow of despair visibly sheltered a man's exposure of a test
Ruthless, vulnerable, and hopeless to triumph the survival of the
fittest

Privilege is always the bright sun that blinds the sight
While the destitute was sentenced to endure all the broken right
Questions follow as to how the church without its building
How the streets are alone, but we hear calls and the screaming

The home comforts abolish the chance for a soul to vanish
But those bed of roses could not feed all the knocking stomachs we
wish to furnish
What is the purpose if we never took chances of mouthing off
solutions
If we're competent and idealistic who inherited Rizal's
visualization

For life is agony, and agony is bliss
Looking through the silhouette of the eye are the waves of seas
Unending, continuous holding a sailing of daydream
And as a chapter closes, a lesson is immersing

Siblings of land with the blood of a hero
Let there be a light to blaze off the sorrow
The sunshine is coming on the long white road
In no time, these night terrors will all get old

Rene Sundiang Philippines. Spare Someone's Life

Carisse Maria Tactay *Philippines*

isdaTama Doggy

Philippines

Novel CoronaVirus 19

An existence we cannot see
Tiny yet so mighty
Prying on humanity
An embodiment of calamity
Sneaking everywhere
Catching us unaware
With death as its companion
Bringing the due of our damnation
A punishment we deserve
Yet to be adequately served
A message from mother nature, saying
"humans, you better behave or face thy horror."
A test to humanity
Testing our unity
An all-seeing eye
Prying on our depravity
An incarnation of karma
An unsealed box of pandora
Known as Novel CoronaVirus 19
Or simply Corona

Adolfo Taroy *Philippines*. This artwork is for our fellow front-liners who sacrifice their safety against the pandemic disease that our country is facing right now.

Hammad Taufiq Covid-19

Neha Taufin

Dear corona,

Sometimes I feel... We as humans should thank you for the change which you brought within these few days.

Thank you for making us understand that no property, no land, no money is important... What ultimately stands along with us is the family.

Thank you for providing us a long vacation to spend valuable time with our dear ones.

Thank you for making us learn those golden hygienic Indian traditions, which we merely forgot to follow like saying namaste instead of shaking hands, washing our legs while returning home, handwashing... Etc.

Thank you for making some of our fathers stay at home and lending a helping hand to our restless mothers... Of course, a huge gratitude to all the superhero dads who are still risking in front line like doctors, armed forces, police, media, social workers.

Thank you for giving some rest to our super moms who have been busy, in preparing our lunch boxes all these years.

Thank you for making my sisters, brothers sit along with me and enjoy those old movies on our television. The Same old way as I use to do in my school days

Thank you for making us understand a simple phrase which my old school teacher taught me....that is ...."*sabka malik ek he.par alag alag he naam*",....no politician no religion or caste system can save up except for our common sense of trusting humanity.

Thank you for making us realize that. Man-made pollution of air, water, can be minimized if we think - it's possible

Yes, we can breathe pure air in Delhi,

yes, we can see aquatic lives near the seashores, yes, we can hear those birds chirping in the morning....

Thank you for making all humans realize that though a doctor is not a god...he can do miracles.... Their 8-10 yrs. of medical study has got some value instead being compared with the - mantras by babes, some roadside quackery's medicines, and last but not the least lectures by great leaders...

A doctor...who is also a common man is leaving all his family life, personal time, eating less, with tired eyes...risking their lives to put a smile on our faces...

Thank you for making us realize the concept of Equality before the law... U have exactly proved the same... You don't judge people Whether they are men or women, a sweeper or politician, a Hindu or Muslim... Everyone has the same lesson

Thank you for making us realize that we are human

Martha Tremblay-Vilao
Quebec, Canada

Through the Window

Through the window
I see
the inside
of
trees
veins
lifeblood
running
a
muted
scream
recalls
life
life
through the window
a reflection
a mirage
water
dropping
from
the
shower
an ocean
a stream
far - nearby
a drum
celebrates
life
life
through the window

inside
outside
lungs
recall
skies
brilliant
trees
crown
raising
heads
higher higher
third eye
curled in
towards

the inside
awakening
I see
through the
window
of the heart.

Martha is Master of literature, master of reiki, poet, and translator.

Grace Tuiza
Philippines

The Equality of Time

This is the time
when life made its turn,
It's different
can you imagine the pun?
We race with all our might
not with power or gun,
But with our life and breath
as fast as we could run.

Nations and countries
all over the world,
The rich and poor you'll
wonder how they could,
Resist the angel of death
knocking at their door,
Not even a millionaire
could have a life to pay for.

Doctors and nurses our
demigods when we're
sick,
Second to God, just their
touch we'll be healed,
How ironic they couldn't
even spare their life indeed,
From this unusual pandemic,
so demonic and wicked.

EQUALITY as people
always claim,

Haven't you noticed
today we're the same?
We're on equal footing
no matter is your name,
Today in this battle we
won't be saved by our FAME!

Grace Unico Tuiza is a widow and a mother of two, a teacher and a poet. She has been writing poems and letters for more than 25 years, She is from the Philippines. The saddest end would be not being able to write... writing is her life.

Bhisma Upreti
Kathmandu, Nepal

Lockdown

When a tiny invisible virus
Chuckled stepping on the supreme ego of human,
The running city stood still.
Suddenly the time died
and everything lock downed
The hurry, the panic, and rushing
as well as dissatisfaction.

The chirp of the birds
rang the morning bell
and sang the evening's Aarati
and the limitless sky smiled blue
like a life's enthusiasm.
Far somewhere like grandfather White Mountain
Stood to line up to give a blessing.

A small garden of my house
reflected a rainbow smile
and opened its arm to welcome me.

Amazingly fragrances of love arose
after returning in the embrace of joyous nature.
Life got life.

Translated by Rupsingh Bhandari

Bhisma Upreti is a poet, essayist, and novelist. He has published nine books of poetry, nine books of essays/travels, and one novel. He is a Gold medalist of the National Poetry Festival. Bhisma is currently secretary of PEN Nepal, A Nepalese Center of PEN International.

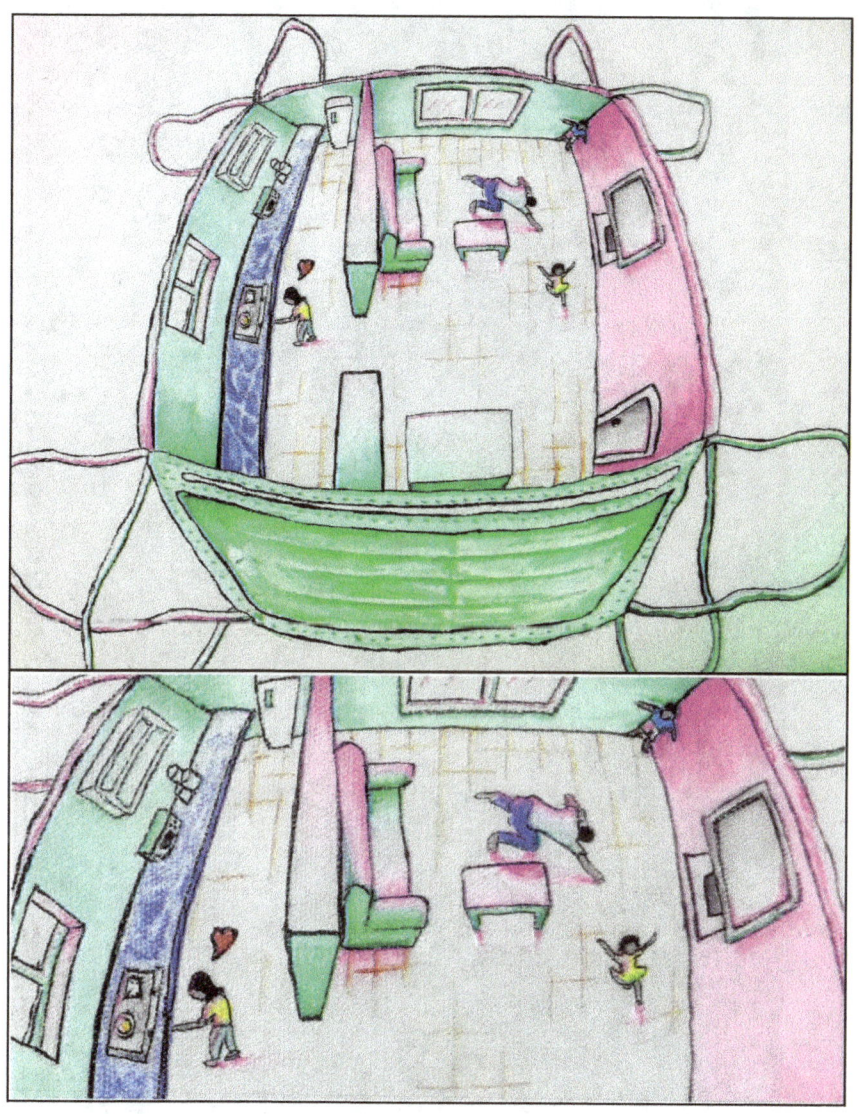

Mansij Varma

Vismaya V Vasudevan *Hyderabad, India.* Vasuvedvan is an art
student at Jawaharlal Nehru University for fine arts at

Laura Wacha *NM, USA* **Shop Till Drop.** Laura is an artist and elementary school art teacher living in rural New Mexico.

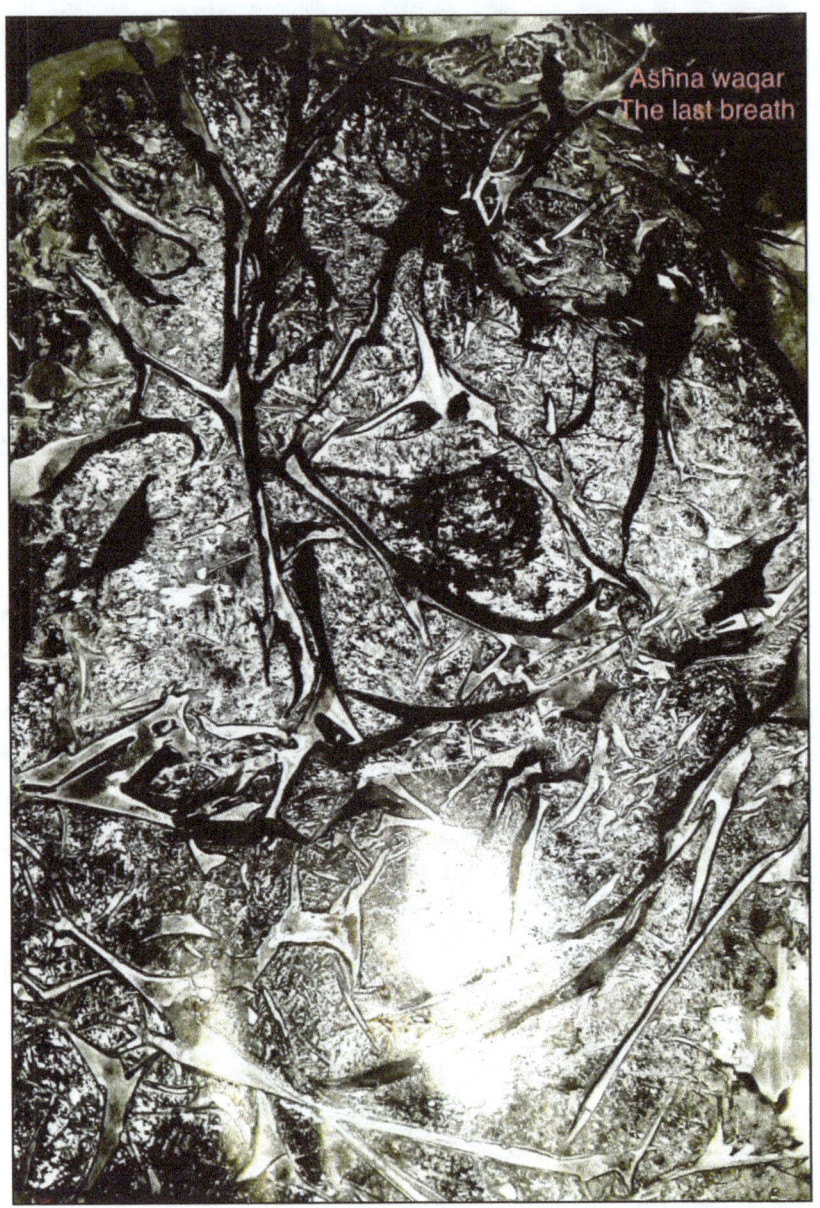

Ashna Waqar *Karachi, Pakistan.* **The Last Breath**

Patrick Williamson *France.* **Open.** Williamson has
notably published three poetry collections (English-Italian)
with Samuele Editore: Traversi, Beneficato, and Nel
Santuario. Founding member of transnational literary
agency Linguafranca

Christine Wishnoff
Maryland, USA

Culture War

A culture war
With a terrible scar.
Doctors, nurses, techs
Knee deep in the trench.
Death takes its human toll
On those who are the noblest.
Heroic efforts to save each life,
Making decisions on who will die.
Watching people suffer
Leaves an indelible scar.
Wounds of traumatic events
Mark future generations.
Health care workers of all kinds
Putting their own lives on the line,
Have become warriors for humankind.
In a war against a dangerous threat,
Larger than the coronavirus:
The battleground of our national conscience.
You can't put a price
On human life,
Without first putting a cost
On human loss.

Michele Witthaus
Leicestershire, UK

Radio Silence

Is it just me?
Or is the atmosphere
somehow denser,
as if we'd descended abruptly
to sea level,
where balls bounce
in slow motion
and come up to meet us
a fraction too late?
And am I the only one
who feels a growing sense
that we're transmitting and receiving
on a different frequency now,
hearing the pop and fizz
of the liminal expanse
between stations,
interspersed with urgent
instructions in tongues unknown;
as if we were refugees
in a place no longer home?

Michele's poems have appeared in a variety of anthologies and other publications. Her background is in journalism and she is interested in ethical questions and ideas around sustainability. She is an active member of Leicester Writers' Club.

Yuliastuti Wulandari *Indonesia.* **Hope.** This art represents the "HOPE" of Indonesian women to end the COVID'19 pandemic, the women in Indonesia are struggling to overcome many difficulties in economic and social life because of social distancing.

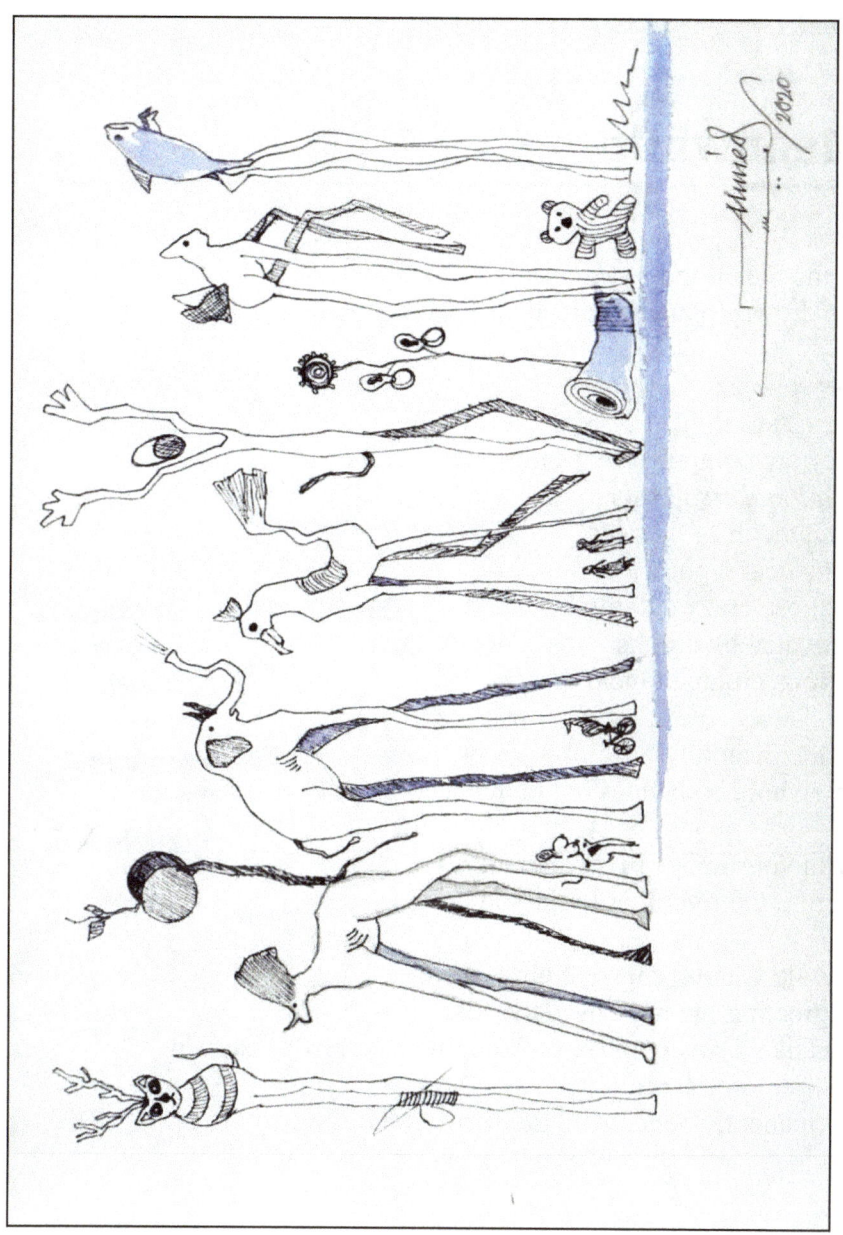

Ahmed Yasin Dance in the Pangs of Extinction

Yuri Zambrano
Mexico

Meanwhile

in the meantime
the drowsy planet counts their lifeless bodies

they pile up
they stack
they are computed by Dantesque machines
dead-makers ghosts
homunculi of disaster,
statistical nightmares
of those crazy dreams
activated by crooks
to reincarnate in lucid dreams

in the meantime
my whole body does not understand forced breaks

with your image in my memory
I cross the river that I told you

the old Charon carrying out Hades,
is greeting me from his dark boat
it is like a *psycho-ferry* crowded with sallow passers-by
Ash-colored faces
permanently dance with the shrillest barking…

Yuri Zambrano
Mexico

Mientras tanto

el planeta amodorrado cuenta sus muertos
se amontonan
se apilan
son computados por máquinas dantescas
hacedoras de fantasmas
homúnculos de catástrofes,
pesadillas estadísticas
de aquellos sueños locos
activadas por facinerosos
reencarnados en sueños lúcidos
mientras tanto
mi cuerpo no entiende de pausas forzadas
con tu imagen en mi memoria
recorro aquel río que te conté

El viejo Caronte, acarreando a Hades
me saluda en una barca oscura
un ferry demencial atestado de transeúntes cetrinos
rostros de ceniza bailan con ladridos estridentes…

Yuri Zambrano is physician, writer and neuroepistemologist.
He is the main coordinator of the World Poetry Festival (WFP),
creating poetry schools and making continuously activism
campaigns around the world.

Tanka P. Bhattarai/ Nepal

PHANTOM OF FEAR

The sound of slowly dragged steps
As if they were being pulled at my verandah
Caused, at once, awake in my dream.
As a dog gets woken up
When a mouse crunches leftover at corner of the kitchen.
I stepped onto the path concretized recently
Where my feet could feel the dew and the dust,
As if it was in a long slumber,
As if it were long trodden by the human foot brutality.

Sensed, simultaneously, an invisible throng passed by,
And knocked me down to the path.
Marching heavy steps with clamor
Leaving an unseen weapon to cause human groans and grievances.
I, limply, stood in fright,
Approached the throng at my breadth.
I rushed hither, thither searching armor
Like what a warrior does
To be protected from being shot at war.

Ran towards me, some visible figures dwelling at my surrounding,
Chasing the cannibals away my vicinity.
So ferocious they were at being chased,
And erected a palace of human disaster.
The weapons of sharp jaws and claws
Gnawed, and gnawed the human figures
Positioned round me ignoring,
And satiated the hunger of human flesh and blood.

I indecisively stood with closed eyes

And arms-folded,
As the Pacific of difficulty stood if front
Making hard to head to my utopia.
A feeble one caressed with prickly piercing needles.
Roared another at two steps back
To reign the world of mine autocratically.
I opened the eyes of my sense
With a strength to combat against,
But they showered saliva with boiling anger,
Like rivals throwing spears at the Mahabharat War.

Cannibals surrounded to make me off,
Coiled all in anger
No ways left to make myself on
Rather jumping over to a ditch, where
I, luckily, got washed up by water flowing.
Simultaneously, neighboring grievances reached my ear.
Awestruck!
They all were bidding goodbye with a challenge.
Out of the blue, senses raised me from the ditch.
I awoke,
The dreamy shadow kept flashing on my eyes.
Television was trumpeting then,
"Wash and sanitize your hands,
 Stay home, stay safe ………

Mahfuza Zannat/ Dhaka, Bangladesh

Covid19 is a Round Trip to Desti

It was 29 December 2019 on account of some emergency I had to return to my hometown from China to Bangladesh. Just before one day, I had
confirmed my air tickets. Filling out all the necessary documents within one day, I had to be prepared for the next day. Things could be more bitter if there were no Chinese fellow who unhesitatingly helped me to hand over my form with my Professor's signature to our teaching secretary in our college. The mentionable point is, albeit we were not that close, in case of urgency, I hardly found any Chinese friend who had ever shown an unwillingness to help me out. On the very day of my flight, It was quite nippy and rainy outside, although I successfully called a taxi and moved on my way to the airport with my baggage. After five hours of flight duration, finally, I reached my destination. In the first few days, I was occupied with my personal affairs. After the new year, I heard about the novel coronavirus (Covid19), which was revealed on 31st December 2019, knowing about this speedy lifethreatening contagious virus I was shocked. Because before my arrival, I did not have a single idea of it. I was worried about my Professors, fellows, and only praying for everyone's safety in China. Being confronted by my family members, I was thinking whether destiny saved me from being quarantined or there is a twist. Meanwhile, in many countries, several cases have been found. This pandemic did not leave any Asiatic country; besides, in the western world, the situation is more complicated and broke the record of the former. On March 6 the first detected case inside Bangladesh panicked the nation and caused several uncertainties. Thus, it made me think of how destiny plans to reach each destination and how it follows its own will to control the earth. Neither it made me quarantined in China, nor did it impose me to be locked down. Instead, it has followed its power of will

286

while keeping my interest. It made my entry possible in my country before the outbreak; simultaneously, it paused my return to China, following us on lockdown in our country. What is written in fate will always find a way to reach us. Therefore, I say Covid19 is a round trip to destiny following my experience. Still, the world is trying to defeat the mystery of novel coronavirus with new inventions and discoveries. We await the next chapter of a new world to restart our healthy life, along with a ray of hope. Zannat is a Ph.D. candidate, Majoring in American Literature at Xiamen University,

Saloni Mathur, India

Mahnaz B, by Ario Mashayekhi

BADIHIAN:

"My brush and pen explain and explore life as it happens. Without brush and pen, I would be in the solitude and alienation that I found myself in early in life as a child. Whatever may affect me, whether happiness, war, human suffering, will be expressed by my brush and pen."

ABOUT MAHNAZ BADIHIAN

Badihian's artistic expression started at a young age in elementary school by writing poetry and short stories and painting with whatever material was available to her. Life took her through many different experiences such as Nursing school, Dental school, art school, revolution, immigration, and motherhood, but she always remained a poet and artist. She has published many poems and translation books in the Persian language, and English. Badihian has been exhibiting her art internationally for decades, most recently with a solo exhibition in 2018 in San Francisco, California. For 15 years now, her life has solely been dedicated to art and literature. Her latest collection of poems "Raven of Isfahan," was published in 2019, to critical acclaim. Badihian finished her MFA in Poetry in 2007 from Pacific U in Oregon. Her poems appeared in more than ten international anthologists.

badihian@gmail.com
plague2020.org
Mahmag.org

www.ingramcontent.com/pod-product-compliance
Lightning Source LLC
Chambersburg PA
CBHW070110120726
47909CB00002B/557